POWER GOALS

9 STEPS
TO ACHIEVING LIFE-CHANGING GOALS

CHRISTINA SKYTT

BALBOA.
PRESS

A DIVISION OF HAY HOUSE

Balboa Press books may be ordered through booksellers or by contacting:

Balboa Press
A Division of Hay House
1663 Liberty Drive
Bloomington, IN 47403
www.balboapress.com
1 (877) 407-4847

Because of the dynamic nature of the Internet, any web addresses or links contained in this book may have changed since publication and may no longer be valid. The views expressed in this work are solely those of the author and do not necessarily reflect the views of the publisher, and the publisher hereby disclaims any responsibility for them.

The author of this book does not dispense medical advice or prescribe the use of any technique as a form of treatment for physical, emotional, or medical problems without the advice of a physician, either directly or indirectly. The intent of the author is only to offer information of a general nature to help you in your quest for emotional and spiritual well-being. In the event you use any of the information in this book for yourself, which is your constitutional right, the author and the publisher assume no responsibility for your actions. Any people depicted in stock imagery provided by Thinkstock are models, and such images are being used for illustrative purposes only.

Certain stock imagery © Thinkstock.

Printed in the United States of America.

ISBN: 978-1-4525-8577-2 (sc)
ISBN: 978-1-4525-8576-5 (hc)
ISBN: 978-1-4525-8578-9 (e)

Library of Congress Control Number: 2013919270

Balboa Press rev. date: 07/18/2014

DEDICATION

This book is dedicated to YOU. My intention is to open up a world of opportunities for you, towards the life that you deserve.

FOREWORD

One committed decision will turn this book into a vehicle that can totally transform your life. Happiness, health and prosperity will flow to you with constant regularity by following the *Power Goals* setting and achieving instructions you are about to read.

Realize that you are the highest form of creation on the planet. No other form of life, so far as we know, has been blessed with the mental faculties that you carry within you every day. An Infinite Power flows to and through you; this power can be turned into any image you choose. Then, by depositing that image in the treasury of your subconscious mind, you will see it manifest in your physical world ... ergo POWER GOALS. Christina Skytt has created a piece of literature that will stand the test of time and awaken many sleeping souls.

All of the other little creatures on the planet are completely at home in their environment, they blend in; it's nature's way of offering them protection. You and I are the only form of life that is totally disoriented in our environment, that is because we have been given the ability to create our own environment. In his classic tome, *As a Man Thinketh*, James Allen wrote "You think in secret and it comes to pass, environment is but your looking glass."

Christina's energy, along with her positive and enthusiastic attitude, is reflected on each page of this wonderful book. *Power Goals* is a clear, easy to understand, nine-step process. You are embarking on a program of self-development and will learn there is much more to you than meets the eye. You have deep reservoirs of talent and ability within you. *Power Goals* encourages you to set aside some of the things that aren't serving you ... those things you may be tired of doing and tired of putting up with. By letting go of them, you will permit your genius to flow to the surface and accept the image of greatness your soul yearns for.

I want to congratulate you for making the wise decision of getting involved in Christina's program. She is an experienced leader and a great career and personal development coach. Pay close attention to all nine steps she has outlined for you to follow.

"No amount of reading or memorizing will make you successful in life. It is the understanding and application of wise thoughts that count." Repetition is the first law of learning. I frequently read the same page in a book over and over again when I know it contains a jewel that has the potential of altering my behavoir and producing an improved result. I recommend you do the same because there is so much information in this book that can help you improve your life.

I am proud to count Christina Skytt among my friends, and I'm honored that she asked me to write the foreward for *Power Goals*. I love the title of the book because, in my opinion, they are the only type of goals that are worth trading your life for, and that's precisely what you are doing – you are trading your life for your goal.

Treasure this book and use it wisely.

Bob Proctor,
Featured Teacher in The Secret and bestselling author of You Were Born Rich

CONTENTS

INTRODUCTION

"Our goals can only be reached through a vehicle of a plan, in which we must fervently believe, and upon which we must vigorously act. There is no other route to success."

— Pablo Picasso

INTRODUCTION

At the age of 30, my life looked to others like "the picture of success" – an enviable career, lots of friends, and a great marriage. But on the inside I was hurting badly. What I wanted more than anything else was to have a baby and the question why I couldn't became existential. Was I not supposed to be a mom? What did life have in mind for me? Was it my relationship that was failing?

For the first time in my adult life, I had no control of my situation. No matter how hard I tried, I could not influence the outcome. I was doing "everything" and investigating all possible solutions through doctors, homeopaths, blood tests, temperatures, psychics, adoption, and eventually IVF (In Vitro Fertilization). But all I got out of it was a horrible roller coaster ride of hormones, hopes, and grief. My mind was overwhelmed with frustration and sadness, as my body rejected one egg after another. I was too embarrassed to talk about it and I never shared how I really felt. I was happy for my friends when they had babies… but at the same time, I was crying my eyes out.

On top of this, I was in a job where I was working 60-100 hours per week, travelling 80% of my time, being so exhausted when I came home that there was no energy left. My emotional life was a mess, strained to its limit.

Now, I was brought up in a demanding family… and all my life I had been driven by other people's high expectations. I started school one year early, and was sent away to boarding school in England at the tender age of 12. The decision, of course, was not mine – and I was totally homesick, crying myself to sleep each night. By the time my parents visited at mid-term, I had made up my mind to go home, and was waiting for them with my bags already packed. But my father ruled that I was to stay. The last thing he said was, "If you accomplish this, you will be able to accomplish anything in life." So I stayed.

I attended high school in the United States, and after graduating, I was accepted as the youngest student to the Stockholm School of Economics – where the highest grades are required. Once again, I was doing everything that was expected of me. But were these my goals or somebody else's? Was it just the fact that, in my family, "everybody" had gone to that very same school, and many of my friends wanted to go there?

I was living a life without listening to my own voice or setting my own goals. I kept on doing everything that was expected of me and I did it without any type of reflection on what I REALLY wanted.

On one of my business trips, I met with a colleague and told him my story. He gave me a book on personal development and, for the first time, I started to reflect on my situation and my life. That was my turning point.

I started asking myself questions like: "Is this the life I have chosen, or has it been chosen for me?"… "What do I REALLY want in life?"… "Is this the relationship I want for the rest of my life?"… "Am I doing work that I love?"… "Where do I want to live?"… "Are my friends really friends that I can count on or are they just acquaintances?"

I finally realized that I had to take ACTIVE RESPONSIBILITY for my life. For the first time, I set goals that were truly my own, not influenced by others. They were big. They were bold. And they were even scary. But they were mine, and they gave me a feeling of power I had never felt before, from just setting goals. So I called them my POWER GOALS.

Power Goals are life-changing goals that lead you to your true purpose. Since I started applying Power Goals to my life it has become truly fulfilled. The first Power Goal resulted in the birth of my daughter, Alexandra – and like magic, I now have four wonderful children. Because of my second Power Goal, I am now remarried and in a true and loving relationship. My third Power Goal resulted in me leaving the corporate world, starting my own business, and now having full freedom of time, money, and location.

But reaching these Power Goals was not only easy. There were clear obstacles along the way. In chapter 7, I will address TURBULENCE – both internal and external. My own turbulence included the difficulty in having children, the struggle with my marriage that ended in divorce as well as leaving the "safe" corporate world and throwing myself into the uncertainty of starting my own business. All of this challenged my old paradigms and in chapter 4, I will discuss PARADIGMS that control us.

Another turbulent factor was to realize that people who I thought were friends did not support me during the toughest years. In chapter 5, I discuss how to create a SUPPORTIVE ENVIRONMENT.

Along with all these challenges, I also had severe health issues and was close to passing away over and over again. With more than 300 blood clots and many months in the hospital I could have given up on my Power Goals, but I was so committed and I was eventually able to achieve them. In this book I address the power of PERSISTENCE.

After my own experience I started sharing the concept with others – using their successes and feedback to fine-tune my system. Now, I have worked with hundreds of clients in executive coaching during more than 10 years and I have experienced the incredible power of setting and achieving Power Goals. I know for a fact that people can attain unimagined levels of success. We are all meant to live an amazing life.

So if you too have ever had thoughts like these:

- I need to find some balance between work and the rest of my life.
- The spark has gone out of my career – I feel like I'm meant to be doing something else.
- I have so many big ideas, but I don't have a road-map on how to get there.
- Am I working towards my own goals, or someone else's?

… then maybe it's time for you to experience the life-changing magic of making your own POWER GOALS.

I will guide and empower you through the nine step process for setting and achieving goals – mapping out the starting point, setting powerful goals, creating a vision, addressing your pre-programming, assembling a supportive team, taking action, handling turbulent situations, maintaining a positive attitude, and celebrating the achievement of your Power Goals.

I will also provide you with useful information on;

- Responsibility;
- Choices;
- Visualization;

- Affirmations;
- Self-discipline;
- Persistence;
- Attitude;
- Gratitude;
- Positive thinking;
- Masterminding

Imagine the the results that would be produced if everyone took active responsibility for their lives. Imagine if everyone was clear about their goals and kept on going and were persistent in spite of challenges. They would stop whining and complaining and just get on with creating the life that they want. The greatest contribution you can make towards creating such a world is to grow in self-awreness and manifest your own dreams through your Power Goals.

Whatever you have experienced so far, remember that there are no mistakes – only opportunities to learn from. As Marianne Williamson says **"As we let our own light shine, we unconsciously give other people permission to do the same."** Allow yourself to shine and make the most of your life.

My driving force with this book is to inspire as many people around the world as possible to have a more fulfilling life. It's a book about finding your true potential, limitless happiness, and full creativity by being brave enough to set your own Power Goals. It is time to start living the life you have dreamed of; the life that you deserve.

If you are not 100% happy and fulfilled as it is, and your way is not making you as successful as you wish, this book will be life-changing for you. Turn the page and challenge yourself into setting and achieving Power Goals. From the bottom of my heart, I wish you great luck with your new and exciting life. Prepare to be successful!

"MAKE LIFE HAPPEN FOR YOU, RATHER THAN TO YOU."

- CHRISTINA SKYTT

1
HERE AND NOW

"To live is to choose, but to be able to choose well,
you need to know who you are, what you stand for,
where you want to go and why you want to get there."

—Kofi Annan

HERE AND NOW

Congratulations! By picking up this book, you are giving yourself the power to get clear on what you really want to focus your energy on and since you are joining me on this journey, you have shown that you are willing to stand up for yourself and take responsibility.

Life is not a dress rehearsal – we are meant to live our life to the fullest; walk it, talk it and share it. We are meant to be happy and treat ourselves well. Power Goals is the way for you to structure your "wants" and give yourself the responsibility to follow through. Only when you have the focus set will it be possible to reach the target.

If you are in an airplane that is about to crash, who will you help first - the child next to you or yourself? Always put the oxygen mask on yourself first or else you may not be able to save either of you. There is so much real power within you so love yourself for who you are and make sure that you are the most important person in your life. Loving yourself is the key to all other life principles. You must truly learn to love everything about yourself. When you start treating yourself well, others will treat you well. This is easy to say, but not so easy to do. That's why this book will be great for you.

The ultimate state to strive for is what Mihaly Csikszentmihalyi calls the "flow state." During flow, people typically experience energized focus, deep enjoyment, reactivity, and a total involvement with life. By taking responsibility for your life, finding out and setting your Power Goals accordingly, you will prove that you take yourself seriously and flow will be there for you to enjoy.

Responsibility

"If you want to be successful, you have to take full responsibility for everything you experience in your life. This includes the level of your achievements, the results you produce, the quality of your relationships, the state of your health, your income, your debts, your feelings – everything! This is not easy."

—Jack Canfield

Most people do not take responsibility for their own life and tend to blame their failures or shortcomings on circumstances. Many people take better responsibility for their cars than for themselves, their bodies or their mind. Countless men and women complain about unhappy experiences in their past. Others are still angry about something that someone did or didn't do thirty or forty years ago. Although it's easier to blame people or circumstances, we must realize the problem lies within ourselves.

Have you been conditioned to blame everything that is happening to you that you don't like on your parents, friends, boss, clients, the weather, lack of money, your spouse, your children, or anything else in your environment? Well, it is time to stop...now. You are the only person that can be held accountable for the quality of your life and for everything that applies to it. If you don't take responsibility for yourself you will find yourself dominated by the circumstances of others.

You have to give up all of your excuses and take total responsibility for your life and your results - which include both successes and failures. The good news is that if you decide to accept complete responsibility for your life, you take a giant step from childhood into adulthood. Wouldn't that feel great?

Our responsibility is to always choose the best for ourselves. If you are not happy with your life as it is now, don't panic. Then...you are just on a "detour." You can change everything you want. All outcomes are because of your old choices, but your power lies within your new choices and it is you who creates your own life by these decisions. You are the screenwriter, director, actor, and even spectator in your own movie...that is life. So be sure about the choices you make so that your movie will have a happy ending. Remember, the choices you make will create your life!

"Positive change occurs when we take responsibility for our own lives. With this new awareness that we are in charge of our own story and can change it at any point, we'll begin to see the world through new eyes and view our choices as unlimited."

—Doris Iliana Cohen

- A winner always has a solution to every "problem" – a loser sees a problem in all solutions.
- Winners take responsibility for how to solve a problem – losers always have an excuse or an alibi.
- Winners say "I will make sure to fix that" – losers say that it is not their problem.
- Winners are always a part of the results they get – losers are always a part of the "problem."

Taking responsibility is the best way to build good

self-confidence and self-esteem. If you take responsibility, you are the rock that you and others can always trust. Responsibility is always a sought after attribute. For those of you with children, the best thing you can give them is to teach them to be accountable for their actions. Ask yourself the following:

- Do I take full responsibility for my life, my choices and my actions?
- Do I never blame anyone else or circumstances?

"I remind myself that I am capable and free, and my success and happiness are really up to me."

— James J. Metcalfe

The best way to take responsibility for your own life is to give up:

- Blaming others for what is happening to you;
- Complaining;
- Justifying;
- Defending;
- Making excuses.

Make sure YOU take charge of your own life instead of life steering you.

Be 100% responsible for yourself, your choices and your actions - at all times.

Method Taking You To New Levels

The Power Goals process is a formula that helps to get you where you want to go. It's a process for self-development, based upon three areas: awareness, acceptance and action. These areas include all of the steps a person needs to go through in order to get to a new level in life, to operate on a new vibration.

The Power Goals Process

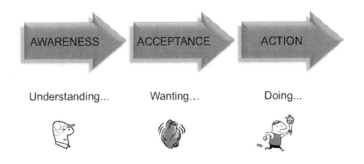

Understanding...   Wanting...   Doing...

Awareness:

Awareness is understanding that you need and want a change of your current situation in order to move to a new position in life. It includes a realistic life overview in order to be able to make desired changes.

Awareness includes the definition of the starting point, the analysis of your daily routine since habits keep you in your current state, recognition that you must take responsibility for your life, and the fact that your choices create your future. When you have created awareness around all of the above, then three powerful Power Goals can be set.

Acceptance:
Recognizing that a change will "cost" you a lot, both habits and money, but still you're willing to accept it and move forward. It may feel like a sacrifice to let go of old paradigms, change your routines, act differently around money or family, etc. The dignity of the "cost" depends on the Power Goals that you have set for yourself. It takes time to learn new habits, and it probably costs money to start a new career, move to a new house, take courses, enroll in a university, or something else that brings you closer to your Power Goal. Despite this you decide that you want to move forward and accept the "cost" it involves.

Action:
Ideas or goals without action is nothing! First brainstorm around what activities are needed for each Power Goal. Then create activities that are daily assignments. Make an action plan with key steps and a realistic time frame for accomplishment in order to achieve the Power Goals. This is when the hard work begins and self-discipline is crucial. Turbulence will be expected and positive attitude is of the utmost importance. Stay with the feeling of "I can reach it." This is your burning desire to succeed. It provides an internal, positive vibration that places you in a desired state of action. Doing it! This is the implementation of action. It's the key to success! First you put it in place, but now you put it into effect.

The Power Goals process is a formula that helps to get you where you want to go. To clarify it even more, you will now be guided through the 9 Power Goals steps to achieving life-changing goals. The process includes mapping out the starting point, setting Power Goals, creating a vision, addressing your pre-programming, assembling a supportive team, taking action, handling turbulent situations, maintaining a positive attitude, and eventually celebrating the achievement of your Power Goals.

The first step is to map out what your life looks like today, your life overview.

LIFE OVERVIEW

Here it's time to investigate what your life looks like TODAY. The first step is to list how many areas you have in your life in order to figure out which are most urgent and desirable to focus on for your Power Goals.

It is of the utmost importance to take a realistic view of your current life situation in order to be able to make the desired changes. Current habits keep us in our current state; therefore, we must carefully analyze our daily routine.

If you want to be successful, you have to know where you are and where you are starting from in order to set out to where you are going. Ask yourself key questions about your life. For example, are you happy with your current situation or do you want it to change? If you aren't happy and would like a change, think (dream) how you want your life to look and the steps you could take to bring about this change. Also, look at your habit patterns and realize that you are in your present situation because of them. Therefore, if you want to change your results, you must change your habits. The same holds true for how you live within your daily routine and what your life consists of. Keep these in mind when contemplating possible changes.

So, what does your life look like today? Get an overview by answering the following questions:

1. Love relationship – Are you in a relationship? Are you married? If not, would you like to be married? Are you happy in your love relationship? Would you like more intimacy?
2. Children – Do you spend enough time with your children? Do you have a babysitter to help you out? Do you communicate well with your children? How is school for them? Do you really know who

they are and what they are doing with their time? If you don't have children, would you like to have children?

3. Parents and siblings – Do you have good relationships? Are they healthy? Do you spend time with them? Do they give you energy or do they suck energy from you?

4. Friends – Do you have time to see your friends? Are you a listener? Do they listen to you? Do they give you energy or do they suck energy from you?

5. Work/Career – Are you in the right place, doing what you love? Do you develop yourself by the work you do? Are you afraid of a new direction? Do you desire a new career?

6. Financial status – How much do you earn per year? Do you have insurance? Do you desire multiple sources of income? Do you feel comfortable talking about money?

7. Home – Do you like how you live? Do you like your neighborhood? Do you like the interior decoration? Do you like your garden? Does your home give you energy?

8. Health – Including food, weight, exercise and medical examinations. Are you looking to create a "healthier" you? Do you desire eating healthier? Losing weight?

9. Fun/recreation – Are you doing what you love? Do you laugh enough? Do you have a hobby?

10. Creativity – Do you know how to create adventure in your life? Do you know how to turn a boring situation into a fun situation? Do you paint? Are you a writer?

11. Spirituality – Do you have faith? Do you have gratitude? What is spirituality to you? Do you love nature?

12. Dreams – Have you taken the time to think about what you really want in life? Do you desire writing a book, sailing around the world, traveling, painting, learning a new language, playing the piano or giving back in any way?

Now you have taken the time and given yourself an overview of your current life and the areas it consists of.

Did it give you any insights?

Does your life include all the areas you want it to consist of?

Or, do you have too many areas in your life that you give energy to?

Stay with me. No need to get overwhelmed. This is an introduction and an overview to what we are going cover in this book. I am going to take you through it step by step. Because that's what I do with all my clients and it works every time no matter where they are in life.

So now, with all that information…are you ready to embark on the trip that will take you to your POWER GOALS?

2
POWERFUL POWER GOALS

"Set a goal to achieve something that is so big, so exhilarating that it excites you and scares you at the same time. It must be a goal that is so appealing, so much in line with your spiritual core, that you can't get it out of your mind. If you do not get chills when you set a goal, you are not setting big enough goals."

— Bob Proctor

POWERFUL POWER GOALS

Only 3% of the worlds population set goals and only 1% achieve their goals. The average person does not operate with goals, let alone with Power Goals.

Now you should be ready to ask the big question...

WHAT IS A POWER GOAL?

"You don't have to know how you are going to get there, but you need to know where you want to go."

— Price Pritchett

Most people have no idea what a Power Goal is and why it is so important to define Power Goals. Many people never set goals, never decide what they want and plan their vacations more thoroughly than they plan their lives. But there are many different types of goals. What's the difference between a "normal" vague goal and a Power Goal?

- Super Easy Goals – that you already know how to reach...
- Easy Goals – that you think you can figure out how to reach...

and the high flying goals that I call

- Power Goals – that are extraordinary, amazing and life-changing goals.

A Power Goal is more than just a goal. It's an

extraordinary, transformative tool for success. It's a goal you set to change your life, attract new opportunities and take your relationships and activities to exciting new levels.

My definition of a Power Goal:

- A Power Goal is something SO BIG you have never come close to it before.
- A Power Goal is something SO SCARY you have no idea how to achieve it.
- A Power Goal is something you TRULY DESIRE and are willing to do anything to achieve.

To clarify it even more...

- A Power Goal give you FOCUS on what is most important to you.
- A Power Goal UP-LEVELS you to include your full potential, instead of just using the 10% that people typically use.
- A Power Goal EMPOWERS you to take steps in your life that you normally would not take... getting you out of your comfort zone.
- A Power Goal makes you PROACTIVE instead of reactive.
- A Power Goal comes from the INSIDE and gets you inspired.
- A Power Goal guides you to make CHOICES to do the most important first, not the most urgent.
- A Power Goal gives you the POWER to create your future.

WHY SET POWER GOALS?

"If you want to be happy, set a goal that commands your thoughts, liberates your energy and inspires your hopes."

— Andrew Carnegie

While nearly everyone has goals, people often have non-specific or vague goals such as…"I want to lose weight," or "I want a new job." While these are a great start, it is important that you choose specific goals for yourself. Power Goals are specific and they will up-level your entire world. When you set Power Goals, you grow and increase your awareness, you have a vision of something specific to work towards, and you are inspired to act upon that vision.

In a study conducted at Harvard Business School between 1979 and 1989, the MBA graduates were asked "Have you set clear, written goals for your future and made plans to accomplish them?" It turned out that only 3 percent of the graduates had written goals and plans. 13 percent had goals, but they were not in writing and 84 percent had NO specific goals at all, except getting out of school…

Ten years later, the researchers interviewed the members of that class again. This is what they found: The 13 percent who had goals that were not in writing were earning, on average, twice as much as the 84 percent of the graduates who had no goals at all. They also found that the 3 percent of graduates who had clear, written goals when they left Harvard were earning, on average, ten times as much as the other 97 percent.

Pretty impressive to see how important it is to set and achieve goals. The only difference between the groups at Harvard Business School was the clarity of the goals they had for themselves when they graduated.

It is almost as if our society is blind to the importance of goal setting in achieving success later in life. If we can learn to set goals and teach our children to set goals, achievement will sky-rocket. From 30 years experience I know how extremely powerful it is to have your own goals and that is why it has become my passion to talk and teach about Power Goals.

How many around you, family members or friends, are clear and committed to their goals? How many of them even have clear, written, measurable, time-limited goals? I presume very few, becuase in general so few people have goals that they work towards every day.

Why don't people set goals?

1. Many people don't realize the importance of goals.
2. Goal setting was never modeled by their parents.
3. Many people think they have goals, but all they really have is a wish or a dream. A goal is something distinctly different from a wish.
4. Many people have no idea how to set their goals. With no direction or instruction on how to set goals it becomes too hard to set a clear, written, measurable, and time-limited goal.
5. Many people have fear – fear of failure and fear of being criticized for not successfully achieving their goals and that's why they don't even dare to set them.

6. Lack of self confidence. Negative self-talk will poison anybodys aim at even setting a goal.
7. Getting discouraged or teased by others when setting goals.

There are lots of people in the world that are really hardworking, but without a direction, without a goal, and all that hard work will then never lead to anything big and fulfilling for that person. I can understand if you have never socialized with people who set goals you can easily go through life not knowing that the skill of setting and achieving goals will have more effect on your life than anything else. If you don't set goals for yourself, you will wander aimlessly throughout the year, and in life. Taking charge of your results starts with deciding what you want to experience and achieve. You must learn how powerful and crucial Power Goals are to your success.

Setting your Power Goals is the first step in turning the invisible into the visible. Living without clear goals is like navigating a ship in thick fog or like flying through fog without a definit destination and a well prepared flight plan. Even if you manage to survive and land somewhere safely, it probably won't be a place you would have chosen to be. Deciding upon your goals clears the fog and allows you to focus your energy toward what you really want. The systematic practice of goal setting will give you the opportunity to take control of your life and you will be able to achieve more of what you want. It will take you from underachievement to success. It will design the life you envision to live.

I know it is possible to set and achieve Power Goals and

I know how powerful they can be since I have achieved them several times myself:

- Going to South America for a first job out of Business School. My Power Goal was to travel and do something different than all my fellow students, by not going into the financial markets. It changed my life, it became the breakthrough career goal and it also opened up the doors for me to learn Spanish fluently and work internationally.
- Finding the perfect house – with a pool (I will elaborate on this later in the book). And then making it happen again, and again, and again. I consider myself an expert in visualizing houses that I want and then achieving them.
- Having children. Despite severe difficulties in getting pregnant, desperately wanting children and doing everything possible to make it happen, I am now the proud mother of four. My children did not arrive the way I expected, but my dream was always to have four children.
- Becoming a professional executive coach. It not only changed my career, it also made it possible for me to open my own business, get more freedom to take care of my children, become financially stable and eventually write a book on the subject.
- Setting my mind on achieving a new beautiful relationship. When meeting my husband, Niclas, I did not just get a loving relationship, but also a balanced partnership with someone who fit my entire "wish-list."

If you can answer "YES" to any of these questions, you are ready to set Power Goals:

- Have you been thinking of making a big change in your life?
- Are you willing to create a new future?
- Are you ready to make dramatic changes to achieve what you want to become?
- Are you willing to let go of old habits?
- Can you overcome your fear?
- Do you want to fulfill your dreams?
- Are you willing to take control of your life?
- Do you want to grow as a person?

GROWTH

**"Everyone wants to live on top of the
mountain, but all the happiness and growth
occurs while you're climbing it."**

— Andy Rooney

The main objective of setting a Power Goal is to grow. To grow is to change and to have changed often is to have grown much. Everything on this planet is either growing or dying. It doesn't matter how much money you have, how many people acknowledge you or what you have achieved in life. Unless you feel like you are growing you will feel unfulfilled.

Setting Power Goals is about developing you as a person. It's about growing into the person, the new YOU, who will be able to achieve what you want in life.

It's not just achieving a goal that matters, but the

quality of life you experience along the way. Achieving goals by themselves will never make us happy in the long term, it's who you become, as you overcome the obstacles necessary to achieve your goals, that can give you the deepest and most long lasting sense of fulfillment.

Growth is the joy on the path to your goal. It will be scattered with pot-holes and hedges, but they are to be jumped and skipped over. Sometimes you will need to detour or re-route, but know that you will reach your destination if only you have your Power Goal in mind. When you get there you will realise the growth that you have encountered along the way. Growing on your journey is the magnificent part.

WHAT IS IT THAT YOU REALLY WANT?

"Setting goals is the first step in turning the invisible into the visible."

—Tony Robbins

Setting Power Goals requires serious thought. What is it that you REALLY want, more than anything else in the world? Is it happiness, fame, power, contentment, personality, peace of mind, or money?

Make up your mind about what it is you REALLY want. Is it finding a new career, a new home, a rejuvenated relationship, going back to school, traveling the world, having your own TV show, losing 30 pounds, getting your driver's license, writing a book, doubling your sales in your multi-level marketing business, or something else that is "revolutionary?"

Although another person may offer suggestions, only

you can make the final decision as to what your Power Goal is going to be. It should be something you want, not something you need, because there is no inspiration in needs. Make it BIG and beautiful. If you play it safe, you will be sorry. Remember, if "they" can do it, you can do it. You need to know that you are capable of doing anything.

Do not concern yourself with where the money, the time, the assistance you may require, is going to come from. Don't limit yourself. Don't think of how it will come true. Just think of what you WANT. What is it that you love to do? Something that's effortless and totally fulfilling? Something you could do 24 hours a day?

Imagine what you would do if you had no fear and all the money in the world. To give you a complete picture of your ideal life, write down the thoughts that pop into your head and never underestimate your first thought. Stretch your imagination. Make sure to not put any limitations on your thinking...think gigantic. You can refine your list later, but be as descriptive as possible when writing ideas.

You can do this exercise by yourself, but preferably with a professional coach, who can guide you through challenging questions. Elaborate as much as you can.

Remember this process is supposed to be fun, so have a great time!

Get your imagination going by asking yourself:

- How would I like to live?
- If I had the choice, how many homes would I have? Where would they be? What would they be like? How many rooms? What is the view?
- How would I like the relationship with my spouse,

my children, parents, friends, in-laws, and siblings to be?

- If I could hold any position I wanted, what industry would I be in and what would I be doing every day? What is my title? Do I own my own business? What type of career would I like?
- How much money would I seriously like to earn per year? How much is in my bank account?
- If I could travel anywhere in the world on vacation, where would I go? What would I do when I got there?
- How many cars would I have if I could purchase all the vehicles of my choice? What make? What model? What color?
- Do I want to own a boat, a camper, a plane, or a helicopter? If so, describe them.
- If I could choose any kind of wardrobe, what would I wear?
- Do I want a housekeeper? A personal trainer? A chef? A nanny?
- Do I have any hobbies that I never have time or money to engage in, that I would like to focus on more?
- Describe what your lifestyle would be like if you could reach any goal you choose.

With all this in mind, you will be able to set your Power Goals.

HOW TO DEFINE A POWER GOAL

**"A goal that is casually set and lightly taken
is freely abandoned at the first obstacle."**

— Zig Ziglar

- In the present tense (as if you have achieved your Power Goal);
- In positive terms (the unconscious mind will filter out the words don't, not and no);
- Be precise and exact (fix in your mind the exact amount you want to earn by doing exactly what you want to achieve);
- Connect emotionally;
- Clarify what date you will receive it (establish a definite date and put a time limit - do not give yourself an enormous amount of time).

MAKE SURE THAT YOUR POWER GOAL IS...

1. Inspiring. A goal can be well defined, but not written in a way that you feel is inspiring; therefore, it is important to get the wording correct and be excited about your Power Goal. For example: "to have the most fantastic job I have ever had" or "earn $100,000 USD per year and feel financially free."

2. Visionary. A powerful goal includes a clear vision. It can be a vision you never believed possible to achieve or something you might already have given up. It is of extra value if your Power Goal can be formulated as a picture or an analogy to describe exactly what you want to achieve.

3. Challenging. It is important that your Power Goal is so challenging it is almost scary. At this point, no one is able to know how your Power Goal is going to be achieved, but you can be certain it will be reached if you are clear in your goal setting. Challenge yourself!

4. Measurable (with a limit). There are many ways to make a Power Goal measurable, such as time, money, a person, an object, or a situation. For example: "I earn $10,000 USD per month" is better than "raising my salary" and "my relationship with X is as great as it was when we first met" is better than "liking X again."

5. Clear. Your Power Goal should be set in a clear, concise and specific sentence. For example: "I have delivered my book to a publisher by December 31" instead of "I have made a first draft of my book and sent it to three publishers." Make it so clear that if someone else were to read it, they would have a clear vision of your Power Goal.

6. Focused. The Power Goal should have mainly one focus. It is better to only include one parameter than many. For example: "earn $10,000 USD per month, in a new job and be inspired by my new workplace" is too much. You can divide this into several Power Goals, "I am so happy and grateful to earn $10,000 USD per month" and "I am so happy and grateful to now be living in my dream home, looking out over the ocean."

7. Distinct. If you have more than one Power Goal, make sure that each of your Power Goals is not too close to one another. For example: "doubling my income" can be too close to "saving X amount of USD per month."

8. Positive. It is VERY important that YOUR Power Goal is set in positive terms!

9. Only your goal. Make sure that it is your own Power Goal, not someone else's. Make sure you are the one defining them, because if you don't have your own Power Goals, you will most likely work towards somebody else's.

10. Present tense. You should write your Power Goal as if you have already achieved it.

And make sure to be happy and grateful for your goal – it will remind you of the power of gratitude and the goal will manifest faster.

Examples Of Power Goals

Financial Goals (income, savings & investments, debt reduction, credit)

- I feel so happy and alive earning $10,000 USD or more, per month by today xx/xx/xxxx.
- Today xx/xx/xxxx, I have paid back half of my debt and I am feeling a great sense of relief.
- Today on the first day of the new year, I have made a financial plan and I am feeling confident and happy to be in charge of my financial situation.
- I am so excited and grateful to have a financial partner to invest at least 500,000 USD by June 30.
- I am confidently checking the balance of my bank account as I make a deposit of 1,000,000 USD, today xx/xx/xxxx.
- Today is xx/xx/xxxx I am so happy and grateful

earning increasing amounts of money, doing what I love to do.

Career and Business Goals

- I am joyfully celebrating my graduation from college with a master's degree.
- I have earned a company award and I am so happy and grateful to receive it today, xx/xx/xxxx.
- I am ranked as the best marketing manager in my industry.
- I feel so happy and grateful to deliver my first talk to an audience of over 1,000 people who affirm my message with a standing ovation, today xx/xx/xxxx.
- As of March 20xx, I have found my dream job and I feel as happy as I was in xxxx.
- Today is xx/xx/xxxx and I skip to work every day, loving my job and my colleagues!
- I am so happy and grateful to have started my own restaurant, today November 1.
- As of December 20xx, I am the number one sales person in my company and I feel more confident than I have ever felt before.
- My company has a 30% profit achieved by today xx/xx/xxxx.
- It is xx/xx/xxxx and I am so happy and grateful that I have sold my company for xxx.
- My management team is inspiring and as productive as the management team of company xxx.

Relationship Goals

- I am so happy and grateful to be engaged to xxx on our 3-year anniversary.
- Today, February 14, I am feeling even more in love with xxx than when we first met.
- Today is xx/xx/xxxx and I am so happy and grateful to have an inspiring and positive relationship with my daughter.
- It's June 20th and I feel grateful that my five closest friendship relations are as positive and inspiring as the one with my best friend Susan.
- It's Christmas day and I have a giving and loving relationship with both my Mother and my Father.
- I am so grateful that my loving husband and I are expecting a baby that is due in August this year.

Health Goals

- It is xx/xx/xxx and I am so happy to have the winning feeling while finishing my first marathon.
- I feel so grateful now that my energy is as high as when I graduated from college.
- Today is xx/xx/xxxx and I feel like a teenager as I can wear a size 10 again.
- I am happy and grateful now that I am at my ideal weight of 178 pounds, today xx/xx/xxxx
- Today is xx/xx/xxxx and I am so happy and grateful now that I have overcome stress and thrive like I did in 2007.
- My feeling of being here and now, focusing on all the good in life, is allowing me to make quantum leaps in life.

- I am feeling grateful about having an amazing self-confidence that allows me to walk on the beach in my new bathing suit this summer.

Creative Goals

- I am so happy and grateful to be an international bestselling author and I have been interviewed on television five times by xx/xx/xxxx
- As of xxx, my dream has come true and I am singing the lead in Phantom of the Opera at xxx.
- On December 1, 20xx my first book for children has been published and my grandchildren are so proud of me.
- I am so excited and grateful that all of my paintings were sold at my first art exhibition on xx/xx/xxxx.
- Today, July 1, 20xx, I am so happy and grateful that I am living in my new house with a garden and a pool.

Making a difference

- I feel proud to regularly give away 10% of my gross income by January 15, xxxx.
- Today xx/xx/xxxx I am so happy and grateful to be an ambassador for saving rhinos, at Kingsley Holgate foundation, contributing to making a difference for the animals in South Africa.
- I feel such pride and gratitude today xx/xx/xxxx as I am walking up on stage to receive my award and receiving a roar of applause for making a difference in the community, running an orphanage.
- Today xx/xx/xxxx I am so happy and grateful to

volunteer mentor at least one young entrepreneur
every year

**"Not having a clear goal leads to a life
of a thousand compromises."**

— Niclas Magnusson

TIME TO SET YOUR OWN POWER GOALS

**"It's estimated that about 95% (of people) can be
compared to ships without rudders. Subject to every
shift of wind and tide, they're helplessly adrift. And
while they fondly hope that they'll one day drift into
a rich and successful port, you and I know that for
every narrow harbor entrance, there are a 1,000 miles
of rocky coastline. The chances against their drifting
into port are 1,000 to one. But the 3% who have
taken the time and exercised the discipline to decide
on a destination and to chart a course sail straight
and far across the deep oceans of life, reaching one
port after another and accomplishing more in just a
few years than the rest accomplish in a lifetime."**

— Earl Nightingale

How can you get what you want if you can't describe
what you want? Now it's time to focus on what you are
absolutely in love with and get clear on your own Power
Goals. We have gone through what a Power Goal is, and
you have been guided on how to investigate what you
really want and how to define a Power Goal. Now it's
time for YOU to set your own Power Goals - to clarify to
yourself and to the world what you are going to achieve.
The idea is to work on three Power Goals at the same

time. It gives you focus. I always tell my clients that only one Power Goal is not enough, two Power Goals are OK, three are a good stretch, and four are usually too many to cope with at one time.

Take your notes and thoughts and define your three Power Goals: Write your Power Goal in the present tense, in positive terms, precise and exact, clarify what date you will receive it, and connect emotionally. If you feel unsure about the foci of your Power Goals, as a rule of thumb, choose one career goal, one personal goal and one goal on how you can make a difference in the world, contributing in some way.

Examples of Power Goals:

"I am so happy and grateful to be the number one salesperson in my company, earning a minimum of $200,000 per year now that it is January 1, 20xx."

"It is December 31, 20xx and I am so happy and grateful now that my relationship with Anna is as loving and exciting as when we were just married."

"It is xx/xx/xxx and I am so happy and grateful to give back to the world by contributing to housing for homeless in my community and getting the wonderful feeling of accomplishment doing something valuable for somebody else."

Notice that the statements are in the present tense, clearly "positive" and there are no negative words. The written goal places the individual in a position that the goal has already been achieved. Live and act the part, be clear of the exact date and amount, and be happy and grateful.

If you feel unsure about how to define your Power

Goals, think of what you would do even when you're not being paid to do it. Think of what excites you the most. Being passionate about your Power Goal will make you happy because it fulfills your "highest needs." Your Power Goals do not have to be about introducing something new into your life. They can be about introducing something bigger.

Now, go for it... define your Power Goals.

Power Goal #1 _____

Power Goal #2 _____

Power Goal #3_____

STRETCH IT

"If your Power Goal is not scary and exciting, then it probably is not a good goal for you."

— Bob Proctor

Now that you have your Power Goals, I encourage you to re-evaluate them one more time. Regardless of what you have decided your Power Goals to be, permit me to suggest that you stretch them. Add 10, 25 or 50 percent to them. If your old conditioning is telling you not to, you know you are on the right track.

Remember:

- Make it BIG and beautiful.
- If you play it safe, you will be sorry.
- And if "they" can do it, you can do it.

THE GOLD CARD

"If you believe, the belief will actually create a fact."

—William James

Once you have defined your Power Goal, write it down on a card (the size of a business card), wrap it in plastic, and then put it in your pocket, handbag or wallet so you see it and touch it all the time. When you write what you want on your card, keep the card with you; keep reading the goal on the card and you will then start believing what is written. The degree of success skyrockets with those who have their goal in writing.

We will talk more about your subconscious mind later on, but understand that your subconscious mind never sleeps. That is why you should also read your goal card aloud to yourself before retiring to bed at night. You can imprint something in your mind that was not true to you, while you were writing or saying it out loud.

Your goal card is a symbol so carry it everywhere, every day. Carry it loosely in your pocket and touch it often. The symbolic value means that when you touch it, the cells of recognition in your brain will be triggered and the image of your goal will flash on the screen of your mind. The picture you hold in your mind will, eventually, be expressed in physical form or circumstance.

The goal card will be your "gold card" and will most likely be your golden ticket to success!

WHAT TURNS YOUR POWER GOAL INTO A REALITY?

The reason Power Goals work is when you develop a

consistent and impassioned focus on something, you'll experience it. Setting your Power Goals is acknowledging to your conscious and subconscious mind that where you are is not where you want to be. Having a clear goal creates positive pressure, which is necessary to move forward.

But there is a big difference between setting a goal and actually achieving it. For many years, I worked at my goals, writing them down once a year, in January, and then reviewing them at the end of the year, in December. Even this was enough to make an incredible difference in my life. I would find that most of the time my goals had been accomplished, including some of the most unbelievable goals on the list. Then, I learned the technique that changed my life. I discovered how powerful it is to not only write down your goals once a year, but to write them down every day. Repetition of the goal creates magic (and results). Your mind will sparkle with ideas and insights. Your work and personal life will begin to improve dramatically. Everything will begin to change in a very positive way.

Be a goal achiever, not just a goal setter. This is what turns your Power Goals into reality:

- Write down your goal every day.
- Carry your magic card with you at all times.
- Visualize what it feels like when you have achieved your goal.
- Believe in your goal and in yourself.
- Create a supportive environment.
- Make sure to have a plan of action.

- Internal and external "roadblocks" are dealt with positively.
- Stay with a general, positive mental attitude.

You know your Power Goals, you have just defined exactly what you want and now it's time to learn how to achieve them.

THE WHY

Why are you setting Power Goals? Get clear on what is your driving force to achieve them. What will make it happen? Why will you do it, without making excuses?

I want you to create a big enough "why" for each of your Power Goals.

1.   Write down all you will gain from achieving your goal – why you are committed to making it a reality.

_____

_____

_____

2.   Write down what it will cost you to NOT achieve your goals.

_____

_____

_____

BECOME A POWER GOALS ACHIEVER

"Whatever you do TODAY, do it with integrity.
Wherever you go TODAY, go as a leader.
Whomever you serve TODAY, serve with
caring. Whenever you dream, dream with your
all—and never, ever give up. You may go down,
but keep getting up—and never give up."

— David Gergen

Your thoughts are dealt with in your conscious mind. It could be said that the conscious mind is the unconscious mind's vehicle for communicating with the outside world. The conscious mind can accept or reject any idea. This is your free will. No person or circumstance can cause you to think thoughts you do not choose yourself.

Your feelings are dealt with in your unconscious mind - the power center. It functions in every cell of your body. The unconscious mind is very powerful and functions while we sleep, It has no ability to reject every thought your conscious mind chooses.

Action is how you deal with your thoughts and feelings and action makes up the results you achieve. If you do everything the same way you have done them before, not much is going to change. Start doing things differently to get new results. If you do what you've always done, you'll get what you've always gotten.

Focus positively
Focus on what you DO want, not what you don't want. I have seen great success in my business because I always declare what I want, and then I focus only on that vision coming into manifestation. In my business, I focus on

the feeling of success and abundance. That is the only feeling I hold and that is why my business has gone from zero when I started at the dining room table and is now projected to generate a million dollars in sales. It works for me. It works for my clients. And it will work for you.

Order is the base
Think of how much energy is consumed when the surrounding is not in order both physically and mentally. Clean your desk and make sure to clear out stuff that is a distraction, taking energy away from your real Power Goal. This can be a simple thing like old photos not having been put into order or clutter in the garage.

Let go of the past
Do not let old conditioning prevent you from moving forward. Remove any resistance that will prevent you from achieving your goal. Many people want to skip over this part, though it is one of the most crucial steps. A good way to start is to write down any beliefs or habits you feel may be holding you back. Remember, there is no reason to feel bad for having a strong Power Goal, having desires and wanting to live a fuller life.

Example of beliefs that may be holding you back:

- "I am not worth it..."
- "I will never be able to change..."
- "If good things start happening, soon bad things will happen, too..."

What beliefs are holding you back? You must truly believe you deserve the positive changes that are coming your way. Do not let limiting beliefs get between you and your goals.

Goal achievers have a winning attitude

People with good attitudes naturally rise to the top. Attitude determines your attitude towards the world and the world's attitude towards you. People react to us according to our attitude. Attitude empowers you with power to change your surroundings to fit what you want. It is imperative that you believe in yourself...have faith in your abilities and feel yourself as able to accomplish your goal. You instantly send out positive vibrations and wonderful things will begin to happen. Self-esteem and winning attitudes help you rise to the top. It is the foundation which you will build upon.

Expect success

Studies conducted of the lives of thousands of successful people have shown that they radiate confidence and assurance. They expect success and therefore, they get success. You can spot these people by the way they walk, look and act. You can feel it about them when they enter a room. They have an attitude which attracts success...they are goal achievers. Don't just feel it...expect it, because you certainly deserve it.

See possibilities everywhere

Believe in your Power Goal and tell yourself that all things are possible. See possibilities everywhere. Tell yourself "I focus on the best in every situation and in every person."

Be a positive self-talker

Treat yourself well to have others treat you well. Make

sure that all the conversations you have with yourself are positive. There's perfection within you so start to repeat this to yourself. Like the diamond, we are all uniquely created. There is no other diamond quite like you. You are precious. Tell yourself "I have a sense of worth. I am valuable. I am lovable and capable." Always talk positively to yourself.

Step up
The willingness to step up and really make it happen is of the utmost importance. Stay on task until the task is finished, go the extra mile, hold onto projects until you get it right and meet good standards.

Believe
You attract what you want to attract, but to do that you have to believe it will actually happen. If you don't have faith it is not going to manifest.

Stop complaining
When we complain out loud research shows that we have already complained 300-400 times in our sub-conscious. Keep yourself on a positive vibration by stopping yourself from this negativity.

Be proud
Everything becomes so much easier if you are proud of who you are, proud of what you do, proud of your products, proud of selling, and proud of what you deliver.

Be persistent
Keep on keeping on. Tell yourself "I persist until I succeed." Program yourself for success. No matter what,

never stop trying and you will win. Go from being a wisher to being an achiever. Determination will get you far. Stay committed.

Success Stories

"You become what you think about."

—Earl Nightingale

If you can define your Power Goal, you can also achieve it. All of these people have!

Dan had moved from London, England to Victoria, Canada because of love. He was a great chef, but did not have a platform in Canada so to earn a living he was working in construction. When I met him he felt lost in his new area and was not clear on how he should proceed in his life in order to feel satisfied with his decision to move to another country. While working with Dan on all his areas in "here and now", it quickly became clear what he should focus on. Dan wanted to get recognized as a professional chef in Canada and he wanted to clarify his relationship with his girlfriend. Dan also wanted to have his own cooking show on TV. He decided on the following Power Goals, to be achieved within a year.

Dan's Power Goals:
1. "By January 1, I have a first class restaurant and cooking school, well known in all of Victoria."

2. "By July 1, 20xx I have proposed to my girlfriend and set a date for the wedding.

3. "I am so excited and grateful to have my own TV show."

Result: By getting clear on what he really wanted and setting his Power Goals, the results appeared very fast. Within a few weeks he proposed to his wife to be, they set a date for the wedding and were married within the year! The result of Dan's second Power Goal became so much more than anticipated. He started a restaurant called the London Chef, which has now become one of the finest in Victoria and in all of BC, earning rewards. He also started a cooking school, a catering firm and will shortly start his own line of products.

The third Power Goal exceeded all possible dreams since he now has two (!) TV shows and not only in Canada, but they are being exported around the world, broadcasted internationally. Talk about POWER!

Martin came to me because he had decided that he needed a review of his, at the time, successful life. He was the CEO of an established and renowned financial institution, but he was not in full agreement with the board on where they wanted to take the business. Despite the fact that he was considered a success by other people, he was not feeling good about his life. We started by reviewing his current situation, giving him a picture of how much of what he liked had been left out of his life. Figuring out which areas he mostly wanted to work on, two stood out – his career and his relationship.

Martin's Power Goals:
1. " I am so happy and grateful now that my organization work like a professional competitive boat." (Martin is a sailor, so to him it made sense to create a picture in his mind of a winning boat that would represent his team).

2. "On December 31, I feel excited and grateful to have a clear game plan for my relationship."

Result: Martin decided that the way he wanted to lead an organization was not anything he could accomplish within the organization he was currently working. Martin was not agreeing with the owners on how to lead the company, so without having a new job lined up he quit. Martin took responsibility for himself and gave himself permission to dream about what type of organization he wanted to be part of. To his surprise, he was offered this new job in "no time" and it was exactly how he had pictured it, even though he had no idea when or where it would be. It resulted in him moving to a new country and a totally new job environment.

Martin's second Power Goal was to find a relationship that he would feel satisfied and happy about. As he set his mind to this, he found a girlfriend who wanted to explore the future together with him. Martin is a very happy guy!

John is a Human Resource professional, working in a large international company. He was seen as a successful person, on the Board of Directors, but felt unfulfilled by how the management team was treating his staff and his department. Historically, John had never stayed in a job longer than three years and the three years at this current position was soon coming up. He was seriously considering moving to another company. John also felt that his relationship was not what it used to be and he wanted a new start for him and his wife.

John's Power Goals:
1. "By the end of the fiscal year, I am so happy and

grateful to defend HR's interest with professionalism and integrity at all times, contributing to the overall wellness of the corporation."

2. "By January 1, I am so grateful that we are as happy together as we were when we went to Mallorca in 2004."

Result: By clarifying his Power Goals, John started to focus on how he could defend his team's interests. He now feels that he is a much more "big picture guy" and he really likes his job. John will be staying in his position since he has now found new and exciting ways to develop the existing team. He said that the outcome was more than he could ever dream of. The second Power Goal was also a success. He says that he is now a loving, present father and husband. His main concern was to "give back" to his wife who had been very supportive of his career. When asked if she could see a change in him, she responded that she now feels that he is a giving, supportive and present husband which gives her the chance to focus on her career. According to John they are even happier than they were when they went to Mallorca in 2004.

Ginny was stuck in a place in her life where she wanted to take a leap and do things differently. Her old paradigm told her she should not "try to be too much." While working with her, I, of course, saw how much potential she had and challenged her to set high, stretchy goals for herself. She did not have the education she needed to get to where she wanted to be and she did not have the means to pay for the education, but she was brave enough to set a Power Goal for herself and believe that it would work out.

Ginny's Power Goal:
1. "I am so happy and grateful to be in the perfect job with the perfect income."

Result: Ginny's own words "Life is worth figuring out and the time spent with Christina was time well spent! It has been a truly magical outcome. The job I now hold is exactly as we imagined and projected it to be. I'm now working on the next step of my journey and am excited to be in this process! Christina's genuine warmth and caring create a safe environment where you can open up to new possibilities!" Ginny received her MBA and is in a great and exciting job.

Roger was overweight and was working a stressful job. He was working long hours, not taking care of himself. His wish was to get a more balanced life, feel more energetic and lose weight. Roger wanted to find a more balanced way to work, making sure he was not spending too much energy on each task. Roger also wanted to become a more relationship-oriented leader, daring to be himself and showing a clear leadership. His role model was his boss, Peter.

Roger's Power Goals:
1. "I handle work situations with less energy cost, feeling like I did 10 years ago."

2. "In July I am proud to act like Peter in his relationship-creating leadership."

3. "I am excited that my health now is great since I have

reached a stable change in both strength and weight, losing 20 pounds and exercising daily!"

Result: Roger created a "key to energy", where he made a conclusion every day of what had cost him energy and what had gained him energy. He went from giving energy without losing energy in meetings with people. He had more energy at the end of the day, despite working at least as much as before and having a thousand responsibilities.

He started exercising, being more sociable at work, and believing in himself so that he could act and become the relationship-oriented leader he wanted to be. He is no longer afraid to be "himself" and set boundaries with the management team. Roger has become an authority, somebody the employees listen to. His own words, in summary of this: "Wow."

Roger lost 20 pounds in 10 months. He started counting how many steps he walked every day and realized he needed to increase in order to lose weight. He went from approximately 5,000 steps per day to 15,000 steps per day, with a constant decrease of his weight. Roger himself became a role-model at work which gained him a lot in all three Power Goals.

Eva is a young woman with a desire to excel, but she did not know how to direct all the power she has within her. When I met her she was torn between working her high-powered career and staying home with her children. She was also feeling that she was not taking care of herself fully, without any exercise or personal development.

Eva's Power Goals:

1. "By January I have identified and made myself ready to take the next step in my career." (She wanted to be ready to say "yes" or "no" to new opportunities, while now she was spending a lot of time going to interviews, not feeling sure of what she wanted).

2. "By the first day of summer vacation I am as strong and healthy as when I met my husband in 1999."

3. "In December, I am a role model at work through my presence in all my relations."

Results: Eva has created clarity for herself about what she wants, to move forward in her career. This resulted in the exact new job she desired. She feels 100 percent healthy. She has organized her time outdoor activities, running and the gym. Eva has become a more present with her family and more caring through taking care of herself. She is a role model in her environment.

Are you ready to start the journey of achieving your Power Goals? As mentioned before, Power Goals are about developing you as a person. It's about growing into the person, the new you, who will be able to achieve what you want in life. No one is ready for something unless they believe they can acquire it. If you only wish for it, then you aren't really committed to it. Become focused and truly believe you are ready to receive.

With your Power Goals in mind... it's time to be creative...

3

CREATIVE IMAGINATION

"It is crucial to have a crystal clear picture of what you want to accomplish. Operate with a sharply defined mental image of the outcome you seek. Visualize your arrival. The solutions begin to appear and answers come to you."

—Price Pritchett

CREATIVE IMAGINATION

We all think in pictures, and then these images control our emotions which produce our actions. Albert Einstein said **"Imagination is more important than knowledge. Imagination is everything. It is the preview of life's coming attractions."**

Do you remember when you were a kid and you could imagine anything, to be anybody? You would pretend to be a princess, a cowboy or perhaps something of the "impossible." And that became real to you. Then we grow up and people around us tell us not to daydream and stop pretending to be something you are not. That is when we forget the powerful tool of creative imagination.

WHAT IS CREATIVE IMAGINATION?

"Imagination is the most marvelous, miraculous, inconceivably powerful force that the world has ever known."

— Napoleon Hill

Creative imagination is the technique of using your imagination to create what you want in life. It is the first step in bringing your Power Goal into reality. You create a clear image of something you wish to manifest, then you continue to focus on the idea or picture regularly, giving it positive energy until it becomes reality. In other words, you focus until you achieve what you have been imagining and seeing before you. A vision is a powerful image of the future and visualizing is the great secret of success, which gives energy to your goal.

Through the years, history has recorded the results of great visionairs since everything ever accomplished was at first nothing more than an image held in the mind of someone creative enough to think it out. Building the first chair... Creating bridges... Flying an airplane for the first time... Creating electric light... The internet... We tend to take our imaginations for granted. We tend to criticize for having "overactive imaginations" or that it is "all in their imagination" and yet, imagination is what sets human beings apart from other species on earth. To step outside of our immediate sensory environment and create mental images of something that is not directly in front of you is a powerful tool.

A vision is a powerful image of the future and visualizing is the great secret of success which gives energy to your goal. Everything is preceded by an image and if you can see it and believe it, then you can do it. This is your invisible power. Don't worry where the solution is coming from. All you want to do is concentrate on building the image of exactly what you want to happen. Practice on picturing your desire as a mental image. The vision or image in your mind must be as real as the chair you are sitting on. This image is going to be turned over to your subconscious mind, which will do all of the work. You must be able to see yourself, with your inner eye, already in possession of the good you desire.

Visualize how your life would change as a result of accomplishing your Power Goal. What would you be doing, seeing and feeling? How would you be feeling if you already had the perfect job, the perfect relationship, the amount of money that you want to have? Identify it and visualize it. Talk, walk, feel and act as you already have your goal in physical form. Be specific. Write it down, picture it, and taste it. Seriously, use all of your senses and get into as much detail as possible. I think a most helpful way for you to understand the power of creative imagination is to tell you about a few of the ways I have used this in my own life.

I know creative imagination works. Let me give you an example, this is a story from when I was very young and living in Argentina, working at my first job out of Business School. After a few months, my boyfriend (at the time) called me and suggested we buy a house in the archipelago of Stockholm. I had no specific desire to invest in a house that I had not seen and I was not even sure I would come back to Sweden, so I passed on it.

Instead I asked myself "What would I want, if I had a house?" I got very excited and specific, wishing for a yellow house with lots of windows, on a big piece of land and with a swimming pool. You have to understand that this was completely "wild and crazy" for a 24-year-old girl to wish for. I got so specific about the house that I started to design the interior of it. With color I made up an image of how many rooms there would be in the house and how they would be decorated. One of the rooms would have a very particular shade of blue, the same as in my apartment in Buenos Aires. Then I sort of forgot about it and left the drawing of my future house in a drawer.

Years later, I was back in Sweden, looking for a house, with my dream house far back in my mind. I found it hard to find a house to buy, because they were all so expensive and not in good locations. Finally, after looking at more than 50 houses, I gave up and decided to live in my parent's cottage. One day my parent's new neighbors came over for coffee. I started talking about trying to find a house and they said they still had not sold their old house, since they loved it so much and were waiting for "the right person to come along." Did I want to come and look at it? I was not so keen to see yet another house, but my intuition told me to go and see it anyway.

Arriving at the house, I almost had a fit. It was a yellow house, with lots of windows, on a big piece of land, with a swimming pool (very unusual in Sweden in the 1990s) and walking up the stairs of the house I found the room with that very particular blue color.

I told the couple that I would love to buy the house, but I knew I could not afford it. Now, this is how the universe works. They responded that they did not have any children and were so thrilled to have found the right person for the house that they were happy to sell me the house for next to nothing. This is a perfect example of how imagining a seemingly impossible outcome will "by magic" make it happen!

Ever since, I have rehearsed in my mind the moves that I would make to get closer to my goals. I saw myself in control, and winning. Did I always win? No, I didn't win every time. However, I know that my mental vision and rehearsal helped me to succeed more often.

Winning or achieving your goal can take time. It took a long time for me to reach my ultimate goal of having children. I had many setbacks and many "bumps in the road" before I was blessed with my daughter Alexandra. It took me almost 10 years to become the mother I so longed to be. I was tested and I managed to stay persistent and not give up. Eventually it paid off – big time. Even better than I had imagined.

Since I knew it "worked" I also started to use this mental rehearsal and "inner practice" for test taking, job interviews, speaking in public, and much more. Any event or scenario that is imagined in detail is more likely to come to pass in reality, or in the physical world. Some events can "manifest" quickly, for example, a really good talk with your child or a business colleague. Other events, such as a trip around the world or a new home, will take more "inner work," as well as concrete action items.

The Power Goal that you form in your imagination is the end result you want. If you are not proactive in creating the life you want, then other people will plan your life for you.

You will often encounter bumps and detours on the way to your goal. This tests your determination and focus. Keep your vision, and act "as if" you have achieved your goal already. Feel and act in confidence.

What have I manifested in my life, by creatively visualizing?

- A family with four kids.
- A new house.
- A trip around the world.
- A beautiful loving relationship with my husband.
- Creating my own business.
- Writing a book.
- A close relationship with my children.
- And much more...

If I can do it, you can do it.

Imagine your Power Goal and "feel it now" as if you have it already. This is the key to manifesting through creative visualization.

You have the key to create anything you can imagine. If one person can do it, you can do it.

Why Don't More People Manifest Successfully?

"The only thing necessary for creative visualization to be successful is that you have the desire to enrich your knowledge and experience and an open enough mind to try something new in a positive spirit."

— Shakti Gawain

You have probably been programmed "when you see it, you will believe it." Change that around, to believing it, and then you'll see it. One major reason that some people fail in reaching their goals is that they lack focus in their imagination. Write down your imagined scenario in great detail along with the feeling that you will experience when you have met that goal. Writing increases the clarity of your thinking.

Learning how to vividly imagine your desired results; attracting your perfect soul mate, radiant health, abundant career opportunities, or building personal and community relationships to give back, is the first step on the path to making them happen!

As Walt Disney said, **"If you can dream it, you can do it."** Remember how specific I was when I imagined the yellow house? I saw every detail on the screen of my mind. I saw colors, I could smell the green grass in the garden, feel what it was like to jump into the pool, and hear the birds sing while having breakfast on the veranda. Get into as much detail as possible in order to manifest successfully.

HOW TO EXERCISE CREATIVE IMAGINATION

"The greatest gift you have been given is the gift of your imagination. Everything that now exists was once imagined."

—Wayne W. Dyer

Now it's time to take your 3 Power Goals that you wrote down in chapter 2 and start visualizing what it will feel like when you have achieved your goals.

Below are the steps to successful mental rehearsal. I suggest that you visualize in the morning when you first wake up, because you are still in a limbo state between being asleep and awake. I also suggest that you do it right as you are going to bed, before falling asleep, for 5 to 30 minutes. Another great place to practice creative visualization is on a plane, a train, or if you are sitting in a car, not driving.

1. **Focus on the end result you want – and you will get the results**. Be clear about what you want and write it down. In chapter 2 you wrote your Power Goals. Have them in front of you before starting. Think of the Power Goal that you would like to happen, a situation in which you would like to find yourself in, or some circumstance in your life which you would like to improve.
2. **Get in a comfortable position and relax your body completely.**
3. **Imagine what you want in detail, exactly the way you want it** - be as detailed as possible. Imagine the colors, what people are saying around you,

how you are feeling or any other detail that makes it more real to you. If it's the adventurous vacation you want, you could picture you and your friends going over some rapids in a boat, fighting the white water. If you want extra income, you could see in your mind's eye rejoicing with your spouse at the end of the year and planning some fun event together. Or you could see a remodel or addition to your home that you've been wanting.

4. **Feel the emotions as well as seeing the pictures** - mental pictures alone do not have much power. Emotion has power! See yourself winning a race with an excellent time and feel the exhilaration. As I see myself giving a presentation to hundreds of people, I feel the confidence and the connection to the audience. As you picture your adventurous vacation, feel the rush of endorphins and the excitement, the freedom and the focus, and the rush of putting your physical body against challenges. Along with the pictures you create that represent extra income for you, feel the stability and safety, the confidence and gratitude, and the confidence in your ability to give value to the world.

5. **Include other people, and actions in your mental rehearsal.** Instead of a static "snapshot" of two people at a romantic dinner, rehearse some examples of conversation that might take place. See the two of you laughing and smiling, flirting and enjoying each other while you have dinner. Rather than simply making an image of a boat going over the rapids, picture you and your friends screaming as you go over some falls and plunge

into the water. See all of you camping on the shore at the end of the day, and laughing as you recount the day's activities. And with income, don't picture actual money. There is no power in pictures of dollar bills alone. Instead picture what that money can do for you and the freedom it can create for you. See yourself, in your mind's eye, enjoying a vacation with your family with the extra money, or playing out in the backyard of your new house.

6. **Affirmations** - keep the image in your mind and at the same time make some very positive affirmation statements to yourself. "I am so happy and grateful to earn xx dollars per year, help making my family financially independent."

7. As a bonus, to leave room for something even better to happen, always end your visualization with a firm statement to yourself: As Florence Scovel Shinn would phrase it; **"This or something better now manifests for me, for the highest good for all concerned."**

ACT YOUR PART

"Dream on it. Let your mind take you to places you would like to go, and then think about it and plan it and celebrate the possibilities. Do not listen to anyone who does not know how to dream."

—Liza Minnelli

Be a movie star. Act like the person you are when you are already there. Get a clear picture in your mind. Be creative, behave, dress and talk like you are the person you want to become. When you enter a room, feel yourself as already having attained your accomplishments. Live the part you want to grow into and see yourself already there. Make up your mind to become the success you want to be and become the star in your own movie. See where you want to be and then be there. Recall the feeling from when you were a child. Be creative. Remember that you can be anything that you imagine. If you can feel and act it, you can be it. Do you think Princess Mary, Crown Princess of Denmark, who was born in Hobart, Australia as Mary Donaldson, always felt like the princess she is today? Probably not. She acted and then she became it.

TELL YOURSELF YOUR STORY

A powerful and effective tool for redirecting your life is writing down your story the way you want it to be. Intention writing is a process by which you write a description of your ideal day or your ideal life, the way you envision it.

Take a big piece of paper and headline it "My perfect day". Write the most positive version of your story that you can possibly make up and write it with detail. Always write in present tense because you want to feel like what you desire is already happening. Paint your picture with pretty colors.

GET THE WINNING FEELING

"Everyone visualizes, whether they know it or not. Visualizing is the great secret of success."

— Sandra Gallagher

The details matter, but what really matters is that you tap into how this full picture of what you want in complete detail makes you FEEL! Build a mental image of your Power Goal and recognize how good the winning feeling is for you. Forget about your current circumstances and conditions and use your creative imagination to conjure up the image of the magnificent person that you are striving to become...then walk boldly and confidently towards and into that image.

YOU DESERVE THE BEST

**"Imagination is the only nation
that can change anything."**

— Anonymous

Do not let guilt get in the way of achieving your Power Goals. Get in the habit of understanding that you deserve to fulfill your accomplishments. Some people tend to feel guilty when it comes to the financial aspect of their goal; however, let it go...you are worthy of money. There is so much guilt and emotion around money, but it's not about the money. It's what the money can do for you. Remember, in order to receive you must give and you cannot give without money. You can't contribute to society if you have no money. You cannot help others if you don't have the funds to do so. The desire for money is good as long as your intentions are good.

Another area of confusion is about relationships. So many people feel that they are not worthy to feel happy in a relationship. That is incorrect. Everybody deserves great relationships.

All people are worthy of special and respectful relationships.

These are just two examples, money and relationships, that can get in the way of your achievements. Expect to receive your Power Goal and know that you deserve it.

VISION BOARD

"You must be able to see yourself on the screen of your mind, already in possession of the goal and you must seriously want it."

— Bob Proctor

A vision board is like a blueprint of your Power Goal. A picture is worth a thousand words. A vision board is a physical picture of your desired reality. It is a powerful technique to show YOU in your ideal scene with your Power Goal fully realized. Vision boards are a highly effective way to bring your goals and dreams to life and keep your attention focused on what you want to achieve. By creating your own personal vision board, you become an active participant in the creation of your future. A vision board is another tool to help you create the image in your mind of what you want. As you look at the vision board, you are imprinting the picture of your desire into your mind. As you focus on your vision board, it stimulates your senses and evokes a positive feeling within you. Then you have both your mind and your feelings working in full force. Both vision and gratitude are ways to keep us on our paths. A vision board is a powerful tool that anyone can use to shape an ideal future through the power of intention and visualization.

How to create a vision board

Step 1 - Create a vision board for every Power Goal or area of your life, so that you can include all the elements without it getting too complicated. Start by writing your Power Goal as a heading at the top of the vision board.

Step 2 – Make the vision board any size - I find it good to hang it on the wall over my desk so that I see it all the time. Make it on any material - I find cork or light cardboard easier to hold up than paper.

Step 3 – Make sure to put yourself in the picture, either using a photograph or a drawing. Have a picture taken of you and create a picture of you when you will have achieved your goal. For example, if your Power Goal is to lose 30 pounds, cut out a picture from a magazine and put your own head on top of that perfect body. This way you will trick your subconscious into working towards that picture.

Step 4 – Show yourself on the vision board having already achieved your Power Goal – graduating from university, receiving your promotion, having lost the pounds you have been wanting to take off for a long time, proud author of your new book, owner of your new house or travelling around the world. Make it look believable to yourself.

Step 5 – Show the situation in its ideal, positive form as if it already exists.

Step 6 – Place affirmations on your vision board - as if

you would if you were making a photo album; "Here I am driving my new shiny Porsche, parking it outside of my wonderful dream house." Spend a few minutes every day looking at your vision board. That is all that is necessary for you to step towards manifesting your Power Goal.

VISION BOOK

Maybe you'd rather have a vision book, so that you can carry it with you. Buy a pretty book that appeals to you, in color and feeling. Follow the same process as above.

HOW WILL YOU VISUALIZE YOURSELF CELEBRATING YOUR SUCCESS?

"If you see you are going to win, you also see yourself celebrating."

— Anonymous.

It is extremely common to forget to celebrate success, just "brush it off" and continue with the next task. It is important to feel the winning feeling and imagine what it will be like to celebrate, having achieved your Power Goal. Just as important as visualizing you achieving your goal is to formulate how you intend to celebrate your success. This will be one of the cornerstones towards successful achievement. By using your imagination, mentally answer the following questions, as though you've already achieved your Power Goal. Include as much detail as you can in your mind.

1. What emotions did you feel when you achieved your Power Goal?
2. Who was the first person you told when you achieved your Power Goal?
3. What is the first great thing you did when you achieved your Power Goal?

Feel as much gratitude as possible, as if you are already grateful for what you have and what you have achieved. There are different ways to get thrilled about how you will celebrate, once you have achieved your Power Goal.

If you are a **visual person**, you will like to receive something you can see to remind you that you have achieved your goal. A beautiful painting to hang on the wall, flowers, cards, plaques, certificates, pictures or gifts of any kind - something you can see and keep the memory around forever. One of my clients had been wanting a specific painting for a long time, so this was a goal in itself. By visualizing herself achieving her Power Goal and thereby feeling worthy of buying the painting and hanging it over her kitchen table, this helped her pull towards her Power Goal.

If you are an **auditory person**, you will like to hear that you have done a good job. Who is the person who will tell you that you did a good job? Who matters to you? Is it your boss or a close relative? Will it be somebody acknowledging you on the radio? A brief phone call to say thank you can be enough or a peaceful day all by yourself in nature.

If you are a **kinesthetic person**, you like to feel appreciated. A hug, a handshake, a pat on the back or doing something together with somebody. A gift of massage, going for a walk, going to a concert or a game, going dancing, taking you out to lunch or dinner or a weekend away with all of the above.

My wish for a perfect celebration is going to a spa with my husband. Telling myself in advance that is how I will celebrate if I reach my Power Goal gets me closer to achieving it.

What will exhilarate you? Figure out what type of person you are and envision yourself celebrating according to what you decide is your celebration. Many of my clients have been thrilled about envisioning the celebration in itself. It can be a weekend trip with a loved person, champagne on the beach, a day at the spa, a painting to remind you of the Power Goal, a specific celebration with the management team (if the Power Goal is a business goal that involves the other members of management), or a peaceful day all by yourself in nature. It can be just about anything as long as it really means something to you. If it is thrilling enough, it will most certainly pull you faster towards your Power Goal.

Your dreams will help you achieve your goal, but you must... change your way of thinking and acting. Think differently...expect that change...

4
CHANGE THE PROGRAMMING

"You are NOT responsible for the programming you picked up in childhood. However, as an adult, you are one hundred percent responsible for fixing it."

— Ken Keyes, Jr

Change The Programming

At any given moment, your subconscious brain receives and processes over 4,000,000,000,000 bits of data. It is the same as 3.74GB of information. That's almost the same size as a DVD, which can hold a full-length movie, audio tracks and extra bonus features. Think about that. Your subconscious brain consumes a Hollywood feature film every single second. That is an enormous amount of information.

The Conscious And Subconscious Mind

There are two ways our brain works, through the conscious mind and through the subconscious mind. **The conscious mind** is the thinking mind, the educated mind, the intellect. The conscious mind includes perception, will, imagination, memory, and reason. It gives us the ability to choose. The conscious mind is connected to the world around us through our five senses; hearing, seeing, smelling, taste and touch. Through our conscious mind we can choose to stay where we are or we can choose to follow the advice of someone who has demonstrated by results, and follow in their footsteps.

The subconscious mind is how you are programmed. It cannot determine the difference between what is real and what is imagined. It cannot reject, it must always accept. It expresses whatever is impressed upon us.

When we were infants we were born without any particular liking to food, any specific language, or any prejudices. You did not form your paradigm or self- image.

It was all programmed into your subconscious mind by the people you were surrounded by. The programming forms your subconscious mind and dictates how you relate to productivity, money, other people and everything else in your life. The subconscious mind consists of the processes in the mind that occur automatically and are not available to introspection. They include memory, effect, and motivation. Even though these processes exist well under the surface of conscious awareness they are theorized to exert an impact on behavior. Empirical evidence suggests that unconscious phenomena include repressed feelings, automatic skills, subliminal perceptions, thoughts, habits, automatic reactions, and possibly also complexes, hidden phobias and desires. The subconscious mind "short-circuits" your conscious mind so that we make decisions we are not even aware of. It is like operating on autopilot. You do it without thinking.

As a child you have no option to accept or reject information that is being programmed into your mind, but as an adult you can use your conscious mind to choose what you accept to filter into your subconscious mind.

The way to change your subconscious is by new thoughts and a different way of talking to yourself. The only person who can change your subconscious is you, by consciously focusing your thinking on what you want instead on what you don't want or don't need in your life.

POWER OF THOUGHTS

"The happiness of your life depends upon the quality of your thoughts..."

— Marcus Aurelius

What is a thought? Thoughts allow humans to make sense of, interpret, make predictions about and model the world they experience. Thinking is our inner communication with ourselves, how we process and analyze impressions. We create our life with every thought we think, every second, all the time. We become what we think about all day long. Our thoughts determine whether you're being empowered or weakened. The most empowering thoughts you can have are those of willingness, joy, love, acceptance and gratefulness. Understand that the present state of how much money you have, your sales, your health, your position at work, your relationships, etc., is nothing more than the physical manifestation of your previous thinking. If you sincerely wish to change or improve your results in your physical world, you must change your thoughts immediately. Nobody can make you think about what you don't want to think about.

Our ability to think, imagine and create mental images works all the time, whether we are conscious or unconscious about it. We can choose how we think, communicate and talk and we can never be anything other than what our thoughts are programming us to be. Our thoughts are like the programs we feed our computers with. If we put "old" programs into our own computer, the brain, we will get the same results as we did before. If we enter "new" stuff into our brain, it is going to make the difference in outcomes in our life. If we choose to put "bad" things in, we will get "bad" things out. That is the reason it is so important to choose thoughts with great consciousness. We always get to experience the outcome.

The conscious mind gathers information and the subconscious mind controls our behavior. Conditioning is a multitude of ideas, which are fixed, in your subconscious mind.

We create our own presence with the help of our thoughts; therefore, it is necessary to "feed" your brain with "happy thoughts," to give you better feelings, words and actions.

Very few people have gotten new results by using the same thoughts as before. If you sincerely wish to change or improve your results in your physical world, you must change your thoughts immediately. If a change is what you want to experience, then it is the thought you need to work on.

In chapter 8, I will discuss more about the power of thoughts and how it can affect your Power Goals and your life.

"We are literally what we think, our being is the complete sum of all our thoughts."

—James Allen

POWER OF TALK

We constantly talk to ourselves. What do we say? How do we program ourselves? Do you put yourself down? Do you tell yourself you are not good enough? If you constantly talk about how "bad" you are, how little you know or otherwise put yourself down, that will create a self-image in your subconscious mind about your worthlessness. Words and how we use them are major parts of our challenge. Words are creative vehicles. We become empowered or weakened by words. We can use them to sharpen our focus, expand our thinking, and transform ourselves. Figure out how you talk to yourself and make sure you are empowering yourself at all times.

WHAT IS A PARADIGM?

"A paradigm is the way we see, understand and interpret the world."

— Stephen Covey

A big part of the subconscious mind is ruled by paradigms, also known as self-limiting beliefs, fixed habits or installed programs. Paradigms are passed down from generation to generation. Our paradigms form our values. We all have an "autopilot" that is geared towards doing things the way we have always done things. What is your autopilot telling you?

From the moment we are born, we are exposed to beliefs, routines and thoughts that our parents carry around. They got them from their parents who got them from their parents. We are also influenced and programmed by the world around us, such as TV, internet, pop stars, teachers, friends, society, traditions, neighbors, religion, etc. You are a product of other peoples' way of thinking.

A paradigm is the pre-programming of the way we are living our life. It is what we believe is the way things should be, and what we believe the world around us expect us to be. A paradigm is just a mass of information that is programmed into your subconscious mind that affects the way you eat, the way you walk and the way you talk. Paradigms govern your communication, your work habits, your successes and even your failures in life. It is the information on "how you should" operate in life. Paradigms are passed down from generation to generation. Our paradigms form our values. Each of us tend to think that we see things as they are, that we are objective. This is not the case. We see the world, not as it is, but as we are conditioned to see it. When other people disagree with us, we immediately think something is wrong with them.

If you watch another individual, you're going to see that they move in action doing certain things. Watch somebody that you live close to when they get up in the morning; there's a routine. It is a paradigm that's causing them to do what they're doing and they want to keep moving in that direction.

Paradigms not only shape your logic, but control your perception, control how you see the world around you and paradigms actually control your actions and your time. Your paradigm controls your effectiveness and all the habits that are programmed into your subconscious mind are controlling your life, your relationships with your children, your health, your productivity and even your income. Each of us tend to think we see things as they are, that we are objective. This is not the case. We see the world, not as it is, but as we are conditioned to see it. And isn't it funny that when people disagree with us, we immediately think something is wrong with them?

To give you a picture of how paradigms can affect you, I will give you some examples. I was brought up with the paradigm that women can succeed in business. My mother was one of three women, out of a total of 300 students, accepted to the most prestigious business school in Sweden. Her mother, my grandmother, told her she should not go there. "It wasn't necessary." Well, my mother made an active decision and broke away from her paradigm. My pre-programming told me that I was supposed to go to business school, because "that is what we do in our family."

I was also brought up with the stories from my grandfather who was travelling the world already in the 1930s. His amazing stories inspired and influenced all of us in the family, but particularly my mother who also started travelling the world. My mother found my father, who was also a world traveler. My father started young, going all by himself from Sweden to Germany by train when he was 10 years old. He ended up living in France, Italy and Australia for an extensive time. Having these two travelers was not always easy for us kids, because they would be gone to Australia, Asia, the US or somewhere far away from Sweden for weeks at a time. I would be home with my brothers and a nanny, longing for them to come home and promising myself that I would never travel far away when I was old enough to do so. Then growing up, what did I do? I started to travel, because that was my pre-programming. Why do I know so many languages? Because my father told me that I was as talented as my mother in learning languages, so I did. Pre-programming. Why did I always think I was bad at math? Because I was told so, and though it was not true that was the image I would hold in my mind and it influenced my entire life. Do you see how strong our paradigms are? These are just examples. Paradigms can be both positive and negative. If you are brought up in a family of entrepreneurs, you are more likely to become an entrepreneur yourself. If you are brought up with loving and caring parents, you are likely to know how to care for your own kids. If you come from a family that has an issue with money, you are more likely to have money issues yourself. But it's not too late to become aware and take charge of your paradigms. Even though you are not a "born" entrepreneur, you can still become an entrepreneur. Even though you come from a dysfunctional family, you can still become a loving and caring parent. If you come from a family with money issues, it does not mean you have to carry on in that family path. But you need to identify and then re-program your subconscious mind.

When you understand paradigms it will become obvious that high achievers are not successful primarily because of what they know, but rather because of what they do. It's their paradigms that produce the results.

What Is Your Paradigm?

It's time to ask yourself about your own paradigms and how they influence and affect your life. Paradigms are not right or wrong; they are just different from person to person. What you need to find out is how your paradigm affects you.

The program you operate with on a daily basis is the paradigm that is controlling you. What program or software are you operating with today? What are your everyday habits? How effective are you? Are you lazy or productive? Do you see yourself as rich or poor? Do you see yourself as worthy or not? Do you see yourself as capable or not?

Is your paradigm holding you back? If something is standing in your way of achieving your Power Goal, it is most likely your old programming.

Your paradigm shapes your world. The glasses you view the world with come from your set of paradigms. The paradigm is your autopilot telling you to do what you have always been doing. Your paradigms control your life. We're not really in control of ourselves at all. If you're like most people, paradigms very likely are controlling every move you make, even if you don't think so. For the most part, these paradigms are other people's habits – yet they remain the guiding lights in your life. Ask yourself, "What is preventing me from living my dream?" Are you being stopped by old paradigms? Do you see... we face a huge challenge in life? It costs us both time and money... and that's paradigms.

When you have identified your paradigms, it is time to figure out which ones help you achieve your goals and which ones have a negative effect on your goal achievement. How can you handle the ones you want to change? We will make a plan for it...

CHALLENGE YOUR PARADIGM

"If you limit your choices only to what seems possible or reasonable, you disconnect yourself from what you truly want and all that is left is compromise."

— Robert Fritz

Why are we following our paradigms? So we can stay in our comfort zones. Unless we really want to change, we all operate in the comfort zone. **"Everything you want is just outside of your comfort zone"** said Robert Allen. You are going to have to get out of your comfort zone if you are going to go for what you really want. When we go after what we really want, it causes discomfort and our subconscious mind wants to pull us back...this is the old paradigm at work. Consciously make up your mind that the paradigms are not going to control you.

I was stuck in old ways of thinking, toxic patterns, and I felt very discontented in my life in many areas, but I was in my comfort zone and did not really want to change. Not until I decided that I could not and did not want to continue with my old patterns, did I choose to get out of my comfort zone. It took guts and it took courage every time; getting a divorce, leaving the corporate world, starting my own business, and writing this book. It takes courage and guts to challenge your paradigm to be able to achieve your Power Goals.

Let go of the past and try new ways. Do it differently than what you are used to. Paradigms are created from something historic. Do not permit old conditioning to prevent you from becoming everything you are capable of becoming. There is no reason to live in the past...think about it. You cannot change the outcome; therefore, you must release instead of holding on to it. Many times the paradigms serve as excuses. If you want results, it requires change. If you continue to do everything the same way you always have, you will most likely get the same results. Do not expect a big change in your life unless you choose to think and do differently.

Paradigms make us illogical, not rational. We think of doing things and then our mind tells us, "Well, that can't be done." To see ourselves doing it we've got to be a little bit crazy and challenge our paradigm. The Wright brothers, (Wilbur 1867-1912) and Orville (1871-1948) did not have any formal education; no money and everyone thought they were crazy. If they had been stuck with their paradigm, they would never have succeeded to be the first ones to fly. Thomas Edison (1847-1931) let go of the paradigm that "it would not work." Due to his persistence, he invented the first electrical light bulb, the megaphone, the telephone and sound movies. Edmund Hillary (1919-2008) was the first one to climb Mount Everest after many tries. He did not give up and was elected one of the 100 most influential people of the 1900s. Just imagine if these amazing men had given up on their Power Goals. There are many others who did not let paradigms control them, which has led to breakthroughs that improved the quality of everyone's life.

**"People do not decide to become extraordinary.
They decide to accomplish extraordinary things."**

— Sir Edmund Hillary

More than ninety-five percent of the population keeps getting the same results—year in, and year out. This is as true for students in school as it is for the person in business. If there is an improvement in the performance of most people, it's generally minimal and not enough to make any substantial difference in a person's lifestyle.

No more effort or energy is required in order to aim high in life, to want a life in abundance and prosperity, than is required to accept misery and poverty. You may even be aware of someone who has experienced a dramatic increase in their income, seeing them go from earning $10,000 a year to $10,000 a month! If and when quantum leaps of this nature take place, you can be assured that a serious paradigm shift has been made. A change in the programming has taken place.

Breaking out of paradigms, or your pre-programming, is generally very hard. But every time you break out of a paradigm, a jump in awareness will be experienced. The jump and the awareness are what will take you to your next level in life. It is necessary to shift, in order to achieve your Power Goal. If what you are attempting to do is not working, it's because you are using "old beliefs" to try to create a new reality.

When you're attempting to change the paradigm, which is nothing but a mass of habits, it will most probably put up a fight. It's our subconscious conditioning that we are working on changing and the subconscious does not want change. The ideas that you're trying to plant are positive, relative to the ones that you're trying to replace which are negative, but it'll still put up a battle.

It becomes hard to change, because our subconscious mind is opposing the change. I know from experience that every time I have put my mind to change in any direction (career, divorce, travels), I have come across panic within myself, because that is when my subconscious wants to stop me from changing. Paradigms are hard to cut loose from.

Our world and our society is right now going through a huge paradigm shift, going from the industrial paradigm to the information and service paradigm. A paradigm shift is a change to a new game, or a new set of rules and when the rules change, your whole world can change.

Teenagers challenge their parents' paradigm. Maybe it would be smart of us, the adults, to try to understand instead of getting mad at what they are doing which is "so different from how we used to do it."

When I was young, I was told to answer the phone with my full name. That was the "normal" way since there could be several different people in a household answering the phone. Today, my children question why they should answer with their full name, since they have their own particular cellphone and the person calling should know whom they are talking to… a clear difference in paradigms.

Leaders of today have "old" paradigms, but the people they are leading have "new" ones. Today's leaders would benefit from learning more about the new type of management and change their paradigms accordingly.

According to the "old" paradigm, written signatures on paper are the most valid and secure, even though electronic signatures are much more secure. Again, a difference in paradigms.

There will be no permanent change in your life until the paradigm has been changed. I have found from experience that compromise just leads to more compromise. You have got to go after what is unreasonable and you have got to go after what appears impossible. You have got to get to the other side of logic, since both possible and reasonable is controlled by our paradigm. Break through the paradigm. You are going to be delighted to learn that just changing a very small part of the old paradigm can make an enormous difference in the results you can enjoy in every area of your life.

In order to replace an old paradigm that doesn't serve you, a new paradigm must be laid over that old one, ensuring that it's sealed from "leaking through again." When you understand how to lay this floor, so to speak, you will expose yourself to a brand new world of power, possibility and promise.

The program that has been installed in your brain can be changed. Investigate your own paradigms and challenge them. Maybe it's time for an upgrade to a new version by installing new software, YOU 2.0.

How Do I Change My Programming?

For a person to experience permanent change in results, the cause of the results must be addressed. Behavior does cause results, but the primary cause is the paradigm or the programming.

According to Bob Proctor who has been studying this particular subject for over 50 years, there are only two known ways to change a paradigm;

1. Through an emotional chock or serious emotional experience such as illness, death, divorce, not being able to have children, being laid off, a car accident or any other severe accident.
   or
2. Through constant repetition of ideas to impress your mind. As a paradigm is changed, the results change.

You can retrain your brain to actually start believing

that you can achieve all of your goals and dreams. It is possible to break through unconscious, limiting beliefs transform your future.

If you start to understand the paradigm, you will understand the power of habit. New habits, a new way of thinking about yourself, the way you talk about yourself and then confirmed by affirmations will change your paradigms.

Now, start by mapping your present paradigms.

1. Map out your paradigms

As I mentioned before, paradigms are not right or wrong, but it is worth figuring out which parts of your paradigm are limiting you.

- What are your limiting paradigms?
- Focus on one or two limiting paradigms at a time.
- Write them down below.

Paradigm A: _____

Paradigm B: _____

2. New habits

Since paradigms are a multitude of habits, ask yourself this, "What new habits am I going to apply to support a change of my paradigms?" Research shows that it takes 21 days to develop a new habit. That's 21 days of staying with the new you, which you want to accomplish to make it part of your subconscious as if it has always been part of you.

- 7 days for the re-programming.

- 7 days to enhance it.
- 7 days to "seal the deal."

As with everything, you need to not only talk about what you are going to do, you also have to act upon it. My habits told me I should get up at 7 in the morning, because that is the time I have always risen. When I decided that I want to achieve more, learn more and write a book, what did I have to do? I needed more time and the only way to create that time for myself was to change my habit and start a new habit. I decided to rise at 6 AM which is not easy and a few times I overslept, but I kept on being persistent. After approximately one month, I had created a new habit for myself, making time to study and writing.

List the habits you want to change to alter your limiting paradigms:

Habit 1: _____

Habit 2: _____

3. Affirmations

To re-program your brain, you need to repeat the new you that you want to be established in your brain and body. Continually affirming something establishes the belief in the subconscious.

An affirmation is a statement that states what you want and describes your Power Goal in its already complete state. Create affirmations to support your new habits. Bombard your subconscious mind with new thoughts and images of all your Power Goals already complete.

Affirmations are short sayings that agree with your desired results. Affirm the feeling of what it will be like when you achieve your goal. Repetition is the key. Extensive research shows that affirmations are powerful and effective. Once the mind hears your voice affirm positive outcomes repetitively, it will begin to believe them to be true. Your thoughts and daily actions will line up with your repeated affirmations.

To be effective, your affirmations should be constructed using the following steps:

- Start with the words "I am…," or "I have…"
- Use the present tense.
- State it in the positive (To affirm what you want instead of what you do not want).
- Keep it brief (Think of your affirmation as an advert for your brain).
- Make it specific. (If your affirmation is vague, it may produce a vague result).
- To add power, include an action word ending with – ing.
- Include at least one dynamic emotion or feeling. (happily, joyfully, peacefully, enthusiastic, lovingly, proudly).
- Make affirmations for yourself, not others.
- Add "or something better" or add "or more."

Examples of affirmations:

"I am thrilled to be driving my new, red Ferrari" (Instead of "I am going to get a new car").

"I have a great and interesting relationship with Walter" (Instead of "I feel good that my son is cleaning his room").

"I am so happy and grateful to be living in my new, beautiful house overlooking the ocean" (Instead of "I can afford to buy a new house").

"I am thrilled to earn 10,000 USD per month, or more" (Instead of "I have paid off all my debt").

4. **Study to impress the mind.**

To impress your mind, studying is most effective. Benjamin Franklin said: **"Invest in your education. Dump your money into your head."**

To change your paradigm and to become an expert in whatever you are doing, you need to challenge yourself to at least one hour of studying per day. If you do that for a year, every day, you will have studied the equivalent of almost 10 working weeks. Can you see how much more knowledge you will acquire than the average person who does not study?

Why is it that only 3% of the population really make it, and 97% are struggling? Well, from all of my own studying I have come to the conclusion that the 3% never stop studying. They have made studying into a habit, doing it every day. Study the Masters of your field. Study anything that will get you closer to your Power Goal. Understand what you are reading and apply it. It is a great way to impress the mind. So study, study, study.

Repetition is necessary when changing paradigms. Impress your subconscious with new information and repeat, repeat, repeat.

5. **Believe you are doing the right thing.**

Faith and fear have a lot in common. They both demand that you believe in something that you cannot see. The next time you fear something say, "If I am going to believe in something I can't see, I think I will flip over to the other side: polar opposites. I think I will have faith that it is going to turn out exactly the way I want."

You can only see one thing clearly, and that is your Power Goal. Form a mental vision of it and cling to it through thick and thin. There are difficulties and delays that are impossible to see right now. You will get through them and you will succeed if you keep the picture of your goal firmly planted in your mind.

Goals are to help us grow. If there were no difficulties, there would be no growth. The difficulties cause you to raise the conscious awareness beyond where it is at, to keep you moving in the direction of the goal. And once you raise the awareness, you can never lose it. That is where the idea that you can't go back really comes from. You cannot lose the awareness that you develop.

Have faith in your Power Goal and let that be your guiding light.

FIX YOUR POWER GOAL INTO YOUR SUBCONSCIOUS

If you want to change your behavior, you've got to program your Power Goal into your subconscious. Repetition causes ideas to sink into our subconscious mind. And it's the ideas that become fixed in the subconscious mind that cause our behavior to be what it is. Repetition is a great key to success.

To fix your new program into your sub-conscious:

- Use affirmations daily. Read your Power Goal every day, as many times as possible.

- Write your Power Goal every day - handwriting your goals make them more real to you. It is a creative expression. Written Power Goals help you stay accountable to them. Write it out a hundred times for the next ninety days.
- Speak your Power Goal every day.
- Read your Power Goal aloud and clear at least once a day.
- All this might sound totally illogical, but it wasn't logical that the Wright brothers flew in the air. It wasn't logic that got Hillary to the top of the mountain. It wasn't logic that illuminated a room. Do you know what it was? It was illogical ideas.

Now that you've decided to change and you're on your way to fulfill your dream, surround yourself with support...

5

CREATE A SUPPORTIVE ENVIRONMENT

"Avoid Toxic People and Associate
with Positive People."

— Jack Canfield

CREATE A SUPPORTIVE ENVIRONMENT

Feel proud that you have created your Power Goals and you have created a visualization of what it will be like to achieve them. You have also identified the paradigms and how they affect you. You know how to empower yourself internally by using your thoughts and your talk. And now you need to gather all the support you can get so that you will not get lost on the way to your Power Goals. Who can support you in reaching your Power Goals?

There is an old saying: **"No man is your enemy, no man is your friend, every man is your teacher."** I am convinced that every meeting is meant to be, for different reasons and learning. The people you know are definitely in your life for a reason.

None of us can be totally successful alone; we need other people to energize our outlook and find the best that is in us. Benefit from shared thinking since it is faster than solo thinking. If you combine your knowledge with the knowledge of others, you will come up with results you've never had. Since the world is so fast-paced, working with others is like giving yourself a shortcut. You can always learn faster from someone with experience. Instead of figuring everything out yourself, you can get someone to show you how.

A study was conducted at Brigham Young University to determine what factors were important in achieving goals, and effecting a change in your life. Here are the results:

- Those people who only made the statement "that's

a good idea" achieved very little success – with only about 10% of them succeeding.

- Those who committed and said, "Yes, I'll do it!" achieved a 25% success rate.
- Of those who set a deadline (saying when they would do it), 40% met with success.
- When they did all three of the above, and then set a specific plan of how to do it, they had a 50% chance of success.
- Those who made a commitment to someone else that they would do it showed a 60% chance of producing a change.
- Those who not only took all the preceding steps but who also set a specific, regular time to share their progress with someone else enjoyed ...a 95% chance of succeeding!

So now it's time to find out WHO can support you in reaching your Power Goals. We will explore the following:

- How to be supportive and good to yourself.
- How to surround yourself with energizers, instead of energy robbers.
- How to create a mastermind group.
- How to find an accountability partner.
- How to hire a professional coach.
- How to ask for help.
- How to build a success support TEAM around you.
- How to delegate.

BE SUPPORTIVE AND GOOD TO YOURSELF

"You do not need other people's approval. Wanting approval is the same as saying 'Your view of me is more important than my view of me.'"

—Wayne Dyer

Who is the most important person in your life? Most people would answer their children, spouse or parents, but it has to be YOU. If you do not take care of yourself, cherish yourself, boost yourself and give yourself support, you will not be able to do it for somebody else in the long run. It is important to love yourself unconditionally. Stop and think about that for a moment.

To create a supportive environment you have to be supportive of yourself. Before we can receive care and support from others, we must first care for ourselves. Better self-care is the foundation of all personal development. These are some pillars of self-support:

1. **Remind yourself of your big successes**. Take time to list them and they will support you and boost you in your future tasks.
2. **Be patient and kind to yourself**. Judgments about yourself are often the most harmful. As Louise Hay points out "There's one thing that's almost magical and if you concentrate on that, it will work no matter what the problem is, and that is learning to love yourself."
3. **Create a sustainable, long-term, effective lifestyle**. Take care of your body by sleeping at least seven hours every night, exercising at least three

times per week, eating healthy food, drinking lots of water and meditating; yoga or something else that will create an inner balance and reduce stress levels. Just like a top athlete needs good nutrients and rest, so do top achievers in any other area.

4. **Pump yourself with as much good as possible.** It is so easy to focus on others, but don't forget to fall in love with yourself first. Make it a habit to be supportive of yourself by going through your daily achievements and appreciating yourself for everything you feel proud of. Appreciate yourself out loud, to yourself, any achievements (business, financial, personal, physical, emotional), anything you feel proud of (exercise, reading, meditation) or anything that you did not give into (eating too much, lying, staying up too late, drinking, watching TV, playing computer games). Do it in the evening and your subconscious will thrive during the night. Don't ever fail to recognize and reward yourself for a job well done.

5. **Understand your own value.** As Jim Rohn points out "You don't get paid for the hour. You get paid for the value you bring to that hour." This quote changed my reality about work and how I get paid. How about you?

6. **"Feed" yourself with positive.** Understand that everyone talks to themselves mentally, so only "feed" yourself with positive talk, positive thoughts, stick to your great ideas and focus on your Power Goals at all times.

7. **Do not permit anyone else to control your thinking.**

8. Give yourself permission to live a vibrant, energetic and engaged life.

SURROUND YOURSELF WITH SUPPORTIVE PEOPLE

"All we meet and all situations we get ourselves into, represent something we can learn from. Everything that occurs is part of a mystical education where we subconsciously are drawn towards the people and the situations that best help us to take the next step on our journey."

—Marianne Williamson

There are two types of people, the ones that suck energy out of you, the ones that I call "energy robbers" and the ones that energize you, "the energizers." Energizing individuals are the ones who, most of the time, look at the brighter side of life. With their positive vibration and positive thoughts they attract other positive people and positive results. The "energizers" are the people who will boost you and your Power Goals with new energy.

The energy robbers, on the other hand, are the people who mainly look at the depressing side of life and focus on the negatives. This attracts problems and other miserable people to them. Have you ever felt how some people can drag you down? They can always find something that is negative about you, about what you are doing, or what you are not doing. They constantly talk about hardship or give you long negative stories about what has "hit" them. These are the people that suck energy out of you.

Energy robbers in your life make you feel more tired, helpless, frustrated, angry or fatigued when you are around them. It may be a casual acquaintance, a social friend, a relative or a spouse and they are not always easy to detect. But watch out and avoid these toxic people. You are better off spending time alone than spending time with people who will hold you back. Let go of the people that do not serve your purpose. You need to find the giving people that want you to succeed.

SUCCESSFUL PEOPLE VS VICTIMIZED PEOPLE

It does matter who you associate with because you become like those people. If you want to be more successful, you have to hang out with other successful people. You are the average success level of the people you hang out with.

We think like, act like and speak like the people we are the closest to. Look for exceptional people with whom you can build relationships. Get to know them and bring value into their lives by being truly present, kind, warm, caring and try to help them as much as possible. This will make them want to be close to you since you become a magnetic, charismatic and an exceptional person yourself.

Successful people shine with self-assurance, they hang out with other successful people and they create networks with other successful people. It will be like a "virus" and you will feel "contaminated" from the good they can deliver.

On the other hand, victimized people are the ones who do not take responsibility for their own lives or their own results. They make excuses for failure, such as:

"I need a better partner."
"I don't have enough money to do it."

"I wasn't given enough time."
"I was too busy with other projects."
"The director/ client/ friend didn't listen to me."
"I had nothing to do with it."
"It was not my responsibility."

The victimized person does not understand that if you accept responsibility, you are in a position to do something about it.

Stay away from people who turn themselves into victims. Nobody who blames others or circumstance will ever be successful and you know by now, as we spoke about in chapter 1, there is only one person who is responsible for your success and that is YOU.

OTHER SUPPORTIVE FACTORS

There are of course other factors that are important to take into consideration, when building a supportive environment;

Strive for WIN-WIN relationships - Value and respect the people you associate with by understanding a "win" for all is ultimately a better long-term solution than if only one person in the situation had gotten his way. Genuinely strive for mutually beneficial solutions or agreements in your relationships.

Find "like-minded" people. A like-minded person is somebody who is mentally on the same agenda as you and will get you inspired. My opinion is that it will boost you to discuss and explore with people that have the same "baseline" as you. That does not necessarily mean they are always going to agree with you, but you will benefit from their creative criticism. It is quite easy to get approval if we ask those who are likely to tell us what we want to hear. If you have created an acceptable piece of work, you will have proven to yourself that it's good simply because others have said so. It is probably ok, but not great. If you are brave enough to ask how you can make it better, you might even get a truthful critical answer and an improvement on your idea or your performance. It is important that the like-minded people are truthful to you and you feel that you can rely on them.

Do not let other people's circumstances and bad experiences set you off - If you are working with a person who is going through major challenges in their work or their personal life, it is of course important to be empathetic, but only to a certain point. When it starts to affect your own life, your work and your Power Goals, it is time to put a stop to it. Maybe you need to find somebody else with whom to work? And maybe that would feel like a relief to that person who is having challenges?

WITH WHOM DO YOU SURROUND YOURSELF?

It is time for you to start looking at whom you hang around and figure out if the people you surround yourself with are supportive of what you do or what you are trying to achieve.

Make a list of all the people you spend time with on a regular basis. Put a "plus" next to those who are positive and energizing and put a "minus" next to those who are negative and toxic energy robbers.

If you look at your life and you find that energy suckers are a factor, it is important to do something about it. If they are people you know casually or have little contact with, you have a choice, or rather a must, to stop spending your valuable time with them, or at least limit the time. It is, of course, more difficult when energy robbers are people you are very involved with, but remember nobody has the right to your energy. Your energy is your energy, to stay alive, healthy and grow.

At the same time, make a list of people who you know or want to know, people that will energize you and can keep you focused and help make your Power Goal a reality. Make a plan about how you can increase time spent with them.

Make sure to surround yourself with people who are supportive and inspire you to be your very best. Associate with the kind of people who can and will accelerate your results dramatically - people who energize you and want all the best for you.

MASTERMINDING

"Masterminding is one of the most powerful tools for success. I don't know anybody who has become super successful who has not employed the principle of masterminding."

— Jack Canfield

One of the most powerful tools ever used by successful people is called the Mastermind group. The basic philosophy of a Mastermind group is that more can be achieved in less time when people work together. Imagine having a permanent group of five to six people who meet for the purpose of problem solving, brainstorming, networking and encouraging each other. During masterminding, the entire group focuses and gives energy to your specific needs.

A Mastermind group can maximize your success, by giving freely and without demanding anything in return. Everyone in the Mastermind group decides upon the start of the group to help each other as much as possible. This means, "the more you give, the more you get."

The ideal size of a Mastermind group is 5-6 people. If it is too small it loses its dynamics and if it is too big, each member will not be heard.

How To Assemble A Mastermind Group

Choose people who are already where you would like to be in your life. Meaning, find people who can inspire you, give you ideas and who have information and knowledge in areas you would like to expand. Consider bringing together people from different industries, professions and cultures who can introduce you to a network of people you would normally not have access to. Preferably, do not include close friends, relatives or business partners. It will be easier to be completely honest and sincere, when there is no opportunity for potential consequences. Win-win is a key to assembling a mastermind group.

Take the opportunity to include new people who bring you new ideas and perspectives. By initiating a Mastermind group you are organizing, supporting and building a forum for other people's growth. Many people at a high level will want to become involved simply because they normally do not take the time to organize it for themselves. The more interesting people you can find, the better.

A Master mind group needs to be a WIN-WIN concept, so that everyone in the group feels that they are both giving and getting something out of it. The feeling that "this process is working and I need to stay involved" should be present at all times. If your Power Goals include starting a business, ask people who are entrepreneurs or good at investments to join. If your Power Goals include becoming a millionaire and you are currently earning $50,000 USD per year, it is probably a good idea to gather people who are currently making more than you. If you are going to work in an international market it is a good idea to find people from different countries and cultures, with insight on cultural differences and market knowledge. If your Power Goal is to give back to society, gather people who already have experience and contacts in this area.

THE MASTERMIND MEETING

- Meet regularly - ideally, a mastermind meeting should be conducted weekly or every other week. Each meeting should last for one hour, with all members in the group attending in person or by phone.
- One person will lead the meeting and keep track of the time. The leadership can rotate from one member to another.
- One person will take notes and share the notes with everyone in writing afterwards.
- Have a pre-planned agenda to follow.

- It is best to have the leader and the note taker assigned ahead of time. I have a Mastermind group that meets every second week over Skype. The 6 members are from Canada, the US, India and Sweden. We all have different occupations and experience, which makes it valuable for us to share information, both on a business level and on a personal level. I find my Mastermind group to be a wonderful source of inspiration and knowledge and I am very grateful to have them. It can sometimes be challenging to connect due to technical difficulties, but it is worth the hassle and wonderful to have a group of people committed to you, without having a personal agenda.

Before a Mastermind group can be formed, each candidate should complete an introductory application. Possible questions:

- What are your three most important skill sets?
- What are your three greatest weaknesses?
- Do you have Power Goals?
- Are you committed to achieve your Power Goals?
- Are you willing to commit to helping others reach their Power Goals?
- What skill will most benefit the group?
- What skill do you need that someone else may be able to offer in the group?
- Will you commit to weekly/ bi-weekly meetings?
- If you had a million dollars, what would you do?

Once you have assembled your new Mastermind group, state in writing a "contract" to:

1. Agree on the mission of the group, a reason for its existence.
2. Agree that each individual member will share their Power Goals with each other.
3. Agree that no group member will disrespect or put down another member.
4. Agree that no interruptions or other discussions will take place while one member is speaking or sharing.
5. Agree that each individual group member will provide support and encouragement, to lift each other up, be positive and inspire each other with constructive comments.
6. Agree that each member must communicate his or her wants and needs in order for the group to help the member achieve his or her Power Goals.

First meeting

Make sure to set aside more time, maybe 2 hours, for your first Mastermind meeting, in order to share a little bit more about yourselves and talk about what you would like to achieve from being included in the Mastermind group. After that first meeting I suggest that you all share your Power Goals for the coming year with everyone. This brings about transparency and it also makes you all accountable to each other to really work towards your goals. Agree on complete confidence, sincerity and honesty.

Masterminding steps

Step #1: Ask for spiritual guidance. "We now ask to be

filled and surrounded by light and powerful spiritual energy, to receive guidance from each other and from the higher power."

Step #2: Negotiate for time. If you have 6 people in the group and the meeting is one hour – each one of you will normally have 6-7 minutes. If not all are attending, there will be an opening for more time. If you need more time, this is when you negotiate to get it.

Step #3: Share good news – 1 minute each. Share a success story. Remember that it can be even a small success, but even that will raise the energy in the group and for yourself.

Step #4: Each individual member speaks 6-7 minutes, while the group listens and brainstorms solutions. The topic can be professional or personal. Each member should be supported emotionally and verbally from the others in the group. Intense brainstorming on how to move forward through expertise advice, good contacts, resources or visualization of what is about to happen as the goal is achieved should occur. The principle is that we can believe for others what they cannot fully believe for themselves.

Step #5: Each member commits to a stretch for themselves. It should be something they wouldn't normally commit to if they were not part of a Mastermind group (i.e. calling someone, creating a business plan, elaborating on a long-term goal, etc...).

Step #6: End with gratitude. Each member of the group

will express gratitude and appreciation towards another person in the group, towards the entire group or towards themselves for actively participating in making the meeting a success.

Before ending the call, confirm the time for the next Mastermind meeting, who is the next time-keeper and who the next note-taker will be. Also, confirm who will send out a reminder one day prior to the meeting. Who would you like to be part of your dream Mastermind Team? I want you to sit down and write a list of people who you want to have on your Mastermind Team. Don't be shy, dream big. Make sure to include people who will really contribute to your achievement of Power Goals.

ACCOUNTABILITY PARTNER

**"Accountability closes the gap
between intention and results."**

— Bob Proctor

Along with a Mastermind group or instead of a Mastermind group, you can choose to work with an accountability partner. The two of you agree to talk regularly on the phone to hold each other accountable for meeting deadlines, accomplishing goals and making progress. An accountability partner can also provide enthusiasm when your motivation is down because of setbacks or obstacles and can guide you or help you to choose when new opportunities occur. The key to a successful accountability partnership is to find somebody who is as interested in sharing and giving to you as you are in sharing and giving to that person. Again, the more you give, the more you get.

I can give you an example of how I work with my accountability partner. Even though we are on opposite sides of the world (Sweden-Australia) we easily talk to each other at least once every week, preferably every day.

We freely share all our insights, contacts and knowledge. Our discussions are based on our professional way of working with clients in our Executive Coaching, which means we are practicing what we are teaching by following up on Power Goals, meeting deadlines and acknowledging progress. I experience complete openness between us and the accountability helps us to take our ideas and expand them into greatness.

None of us can be totally successful alone; we need other people to energize our outlook and find the best that is in us. That is what an accountability partner can do for you!

Who would you like to have as your dream accountability partner? I want you to sit down and list 3-5 people who you would like to approach, asking them for the honorable task of being your accountability partner. Let them know that you are both meant to give and get support from each other, on a daily or weekly basis. Don't be shy, think big. Make sure to only ask a person who will really contribute to your achievement of Power Goals.

COACHING

"Coaches have the ability to view things from afar in what some call 'helicopter vision' - and to shed new light on difficult situations, often they can act as a sounding board through tough decisions, help sharpen skills, motivate."

— CFO Magazine

Coaching is a process of improving personal performance. The definition by the International Coach Federation is **"A professional partnership between a qualified coach and an individual that support the achievement of extraordinary results, based on goals set by the individual."** To accelerate your success, hire a professional coach. A professional coach will help you clarify your Power Goals, set up a plan of action and support you by keeping you focused as well as enhancing the good patterns you have and training you in new ways of working.

A coach will see the potential that you don't yet see in yourself. You will receive ongoing support, detailed action plans, constructive feedback and personal accountability. Your commitment, enthusiasm and belief in your abilities will increase exponentially.

So, if I have an accountability partner, why would I need the services of a coach? The answer is they are both of value, but in different ways. An accountability partner holds you accountable for a particular goal; whereas, a coach improves your performance and helps you attain success. Working with a professional coach is like getting several professionals in one person.

Your coach should take on several roles in helping you towards your Power Goals, acting as:

The Mentor – who helps you clarify and create inspirational Power Goals, sees your full potential and believes in you. A person you can also seek for advice.

The Project Manager – helps you set up strategies, create action plans, puts up control points for your achievements and monitors your progress.

The Personal Trainer (PT) – who will encourage you, challenge you, keep you focused and on the right track towards your Power Goals. The PT will also give you objective feedback on your strengths, patterns and personal traits. The PT will make you aware of what you need to alter to move you faster towards your Power Goals.

The Neutral Partner – A good professional coach will be committed to you, your development and your objectives without having a personal agenda.

Confidentiality – is of course mandatory Make sure your coach is committed to 100% confidentiality.

I know how valuable it is to have a coach since I, myself, have had several personal coaches who have helped me achieve my own Power Goals. Most coaching clients are smart people. They know they are capable of achieving a lot, but they also know it is invaluable accessing someone who will keep them on track, wants all the best for the client, someone to talk with where the conversation is totally confidential, and someone who can be objective, honest and constructive about what you are facing.

Coaching is for you if you are willing to:

- Grow (personal development);
- Acquire personal insights;
- Keep focused on your top priorities;
- Determine specific action steps;
- Value feedback;
- Value results;
- Achieve balance in your life at the same time as you accomplish your Power Goals.

Since 2002, I am a trained professional coach. I soon discovered what an amazing tool coaching is to help clients get to where they want to be. I got interested in learning if this could be powerful for business purposes and I now combine my coaching skills and my business background, working mainly with top executives around the world where goals and results are the "only thing that counts." I have learned and realized that my coaching style is also applicable to everyone who wants to set and achieve life changing goals, in any area of life.

How to find a coach

Ask yourself the following questions;

1. What type of coach would be the most helpful to you and your achievement? A life coach, career coach or executive coach?
2. Could anybody in your circle of friends or any colleague at work advise you on a good coach?
3. Do you want a coach that you meet with on a

regular basis or a coach that coaches you via phone or Skype?

4. Make sure it is a coach who will challenge you, for you to reach your full potential.

5. Take your time to read through the biographies of the coaches you find to make sure you find the coach most suited to you and your intended goals and objectives.

6. The vast majority of coaches offer a free consultation. That means that you get a chance to speak to your coach before paying for sessions. Your consultation is a great opportunity for you to learn about your coach, to ask them questions, and to see if they're a good fit for you.

7. Make sure to ask questions. All good coaches will welcome your questions and queries about their qualifications.

8. Ask for references.

9. Let the coach explain their coaching style and be aware of how that resonates with you.

10. If you feel a genuine connection with your coach, you'll also want to make sure that you trust them and feel comfortable. To get the most effective results, you'll need to be able to be completely open and honest with this person, so that they can speak to whatever core issues you might have. The more you can let your guard down and just be your normal, natural self, the more your coach will be able to work with the "real you."

11. Trust your intuition.

After you have found yourself a coach the next

question will probably be, "will I be able to afford it?" You must view this as an investment in yourself, not a cost. People are often willing to invest money in their car or their house without hesitating, to keep up the value. This investment should be the way to keep up the value of YOU. Because you are worth it!

ASKING FOR HELP

Many times we don't ask for help when we need it even though others have offered. To be successful in achieving your Power Goals you must be able to comfortably ask for what you want from already successful people. Asking for help is essential. If you ask successful people how they got to where they are, they knew when and how to ask the right questions so they could gather the right information, build their reputation, seek useful referrals, generate new business, and expand their audience or customer base.

The simple act of asking is critical to success. Yet many people don't do it because they falsely believe that asking implies weakness and sets one up for potential rejection. Asking for help is not a sign of weakness, but an openness to learn from others and being smart, taking advantage of other people's experience and knowledge. By asking others for help you will reach your Power Goals faster.

1. **Ask for Information.** You can never have too much information. Ask questions starting with the words who, why, what, where, when and how to obtain the information you need.

2. **Ask for Referrals.** It is a habit that will dramatically

increase your success. Like any other habit, the more you do it, the easier it becomes.

3. **Ask for Written Endorsements.** The best time to ask is right after you have provided excellent service, gone the extra mile to help out, or in any other way made somebody really happy. Simply ask if this person would be willing to give you a testimonial about the value of your product or service, plus any other helpful comments.

How To Ask

The first stumbling block for most people is knowing how to ask. According to Jack Canfield, here are five tips to improve the way you ask to achieve results:

- **Ask Clearly;**
- **Ask with Confidence;**
- **Ask Consistently**: be persistent and do not give up just because they said "no" the first time;
- **Ask Creatively**: ask in an unusual way;
- **Ask Sincerely:** Sincerity means dropping the image facade and being vulnerable.

When you really need help, people will respond.

Connect With People

We live in a connected world. Connect with people who can help you. The social web has demolished barriers between you and the expertise you need. It empowers you to ask friends of friends if they can offer advice, make introductions and share experiences. You can support each other, learn from each other and do business with each other.

BUILD A SUCCESS SUPPORT TEAM

TEAM stands for "Together Each Achieves More." We all need a TEAM, to combine the strengths of people through positive teamwork, so as to achieve goals no one person could have done alone. We live in a very complex world. That is why every high achiever has a powerful TEAM of personal advisors to turn to for assistance, advice, and support. There are people in the world who love to do what you do not like to do at all. They often do a much better job than you would or could yourself; so leave it to them so that you can focus on your core.

The world's greatest business professionals, athletes, and entertainers all have people who handle their everyday life in order for them to be able to focus on what they do best. The best part is that we do not have to hire all the people we have on our TEAM. I, myself, am not good or even interested in bookkeeping or IT, so I have great people doing that for me. They are part of my TEAM.

For example, if your Power Goal is to become a professional speaker with your own website, to support this, you will need:

- A web-designer;
- Somebody setting up your speaking engagements;
- A marketing professional;
- A professional coach – for personal development support;

- Financial services.

It is not just the traditional roles of a company that will become your TEAM. It is who you need to include to feel good and create the best of you. Your TEAM could also include any of the following: a reliable banker, a lawyer, an accountant, your doctor, a dentist, a qualified nutritionist, a baby sitter, a psychologist, your personal trainer or a massage therapist. Massage is essential for me. To feel good both physically and mentally, I need a regular massages. Every week I hire a massage therapist and I pay her. I feel that she is part of my TEAM.

Your TEAM could also be your parents, your best friends, your sports coach, or your counselor.

Make sure that your TEAM members are clear about what you expect from them and that you are clear about what they expect from you. Once you have chosen your TEAM members, trust them - full stop.

DELEGATE

You need to understand and accept that it will often take at least twice as long to delegate a repeating task the first time as it would to do it yourself. However, once you delegate something successfully, it will be off your plate forever.

You must also accept that many delegated tasks may not get done as well as if you did them yourself. Although this isn't acceptable for some areas (e.g., providing a service to a customer), for others (e.g., reordering supplies, completing paperwork), good enough is good enough.

Effective delegation makes you replaceable, and

although it sounds a bit strange, this is what you want. It allows you to spend time growing, rather than simply maintaining your business. You can spend less time working and take real vacations. It also makes your business attractive to buyers, which is particularly important if your end vision is to sell your company.

You need to focus only on the items that add the most value to achieving your Power goals. In general, these are the things that you, and only you, are capable of doing. You should delegate the rest. It is often hard at first to delegate because most people want to control everything themselves.

To achieve your end vision, you must delegate. Consider Steve Jobs. He clearly didn't create the prototype for the iPod, nor did he manage the manufacturing, marketing, or customer service. Neither did Bill Gates. He clearly didn't write the code for all of Microsoft's products. And how could Branson possibly manage nearly 50 companies at once without delegation? Delegating tasks to others can save you a great deal of time and allow you to focus that time on the highest value-added tasks.

However, when done incorrectly, delegating results in things not getting done or getting done poorly, which is when you end up spending more time and energy than you have. This is why it's critical to delegate properly.

Pareto's Principle or Pareto's Law, as it is sometimes called, can be a very effective tool to help you manage effectively. According to the Pareto Principle, the 80/20 rule means that in anything 20 percent are vital and 80 percent are trivial. Project Managers know that 20 percent of the work (the first 10 percent and the last 10 percent) consume 80 percent of your time and resources. You can apply the 80/20 rule to almost anything, from the science of management to the physical world. Also 80 percent of your sales will come from 20 percent of your sales staff. Twenty percent of your staff will cause 80 percent of your problems, but another 20 percent of your staff will provide 80 percent of your production. It works both ways. Identify your top 20 percent and delegate the rest. You need a way to determine what the key things are on which you should be spending your time. In the case of your focus, the Pareto Principle says that 20 percent of your efforts (e.g., your customers) yield 80 percent of the results you achieve (e.g. total company sales). Therefore, the key is to identify what this 20 percent of your work is and do more of it (and delegate the 80 percent).

The first way to determine which 20 percent of work you do yields 80 percent of the results is to think back. What were the most important projects you completed last year that propelled you forward? Your answers will include the types of projects that belong in your top 20 percent and which you should continue to do. The second way to determine your top tasks to perform is to review your to-do list and consider the following questions when reviewing each item:

- Does that activity really add value to your company or your Power Goal?
- Are you really great at performing that task?
- Is there somebody else who can do it better, as well as, or nearly as well as you at completing the task?

A great way to determine which tasks are not in your top 20 percent is to keep a running list of low-value tasks. To begin, you can't do work yourself that you could hire someone to do for a low $ an hour. As you go through your days, write down all the tasks you perform that fall into this category. The next step in the process is to delegate the lowest value uses to others.

Using the following steps will help you do so:

1. Identify the Right Person for Delegation

This person might be an employee of your company or an outsourced individual or firm. The right person is the one who has the requisite skill set to do the task and the ability to complete the project within the appropriate timeline. Your employees should maintain daily and weekly to-do lists. This way, you can review those lists to identify which employees have the ability to tackle the project to be delegated.

2. Clearly Define the Project

The next step is clearly to define the task, the deliverables, the completion date, and why the project needs to be done. If you rush through this step and simply say, "do this by this date" you will get poor results. Be clear on your expectation.

3. Discuss the Plan of Action

You need to discuss the plan of action: Specifically, how the person in charge of completing the task can accomplish it. Of key importance here is that you don't want to delegate a task (e.g., email this report today), but rather a process (e.g., email all the reports I have from now on). Therefore, even when delegating a seemingly simple task such as sending emails, you need to discuss the plan. For example, how often do you need reports emailed?

How quickly must they be emailed once you create them? What must be done after sending it? You want to spend time detailing and documenting how the delegated task should be performed.

4. Ask Them to Repeat Back the Plan

Next, have the person to whom you delegate repeat the task and deliver it back to you to ensure their complete comprehension. Most people will nod and say, "Yes, I get it"—that is, until you ask them to repeat your directions back, and they get them wrong. Have the person repeat all of your directions back to you until the directions are right.

5. Guidance

When you delegate long-term tasks you need to monitor its progress and provide guidance. Ideally, you identified project milestones to ensure the project stays on track when initially discussing the plan. To ensure projects are completed properly, mark those milestones on your calendar and monitor so that results are delivered on time. If they are not, be sure to immediately alert that he or she has fallen behind. Meet with the person periodically to provide guidance.

6. Feedback

The final step to effective delegation is to evaluate performance. Most people skip this critical step and suffer as a result. Here's why: If somebody does an "inferior" job the first time they perform a task that you delegate, how do you think they'll perform the next time they do it? Are they going to magically do a "superior" job the next time? No, in fact, the next time they will do an "inferior" job because they think that job is good enough. This is why providing feedback and evaluating performance allows you to get the best results from those to whom you delegate. Even if they did a great job, you need to explain why they did a great job so that they know how to repeat this performance in the future. You need to explain if there was room for improvement. People generally appreciate slightly negative feedback versus no feedback at all. So, explain the good and the bad, and you'll get increasingly better results on the tasks you delegate to that person.

7. Appreciation

Positive reinforcement makes it better for everyone involved. How does the person you have delegated to like to be thanked? Written, spoken, flowers, or official thanks? Find out what works best for the person and you will get even better results in the future. Not taking people for granted is a key to success. Have you ever heard of anyone complaining about receiving too much positive feedback?

**You deserve to live a full life, but there's a catch: to get it you are going to have to demand more yourself. So...
Now it's time to slip into action...**

6
ACTION

"The secret of getting ahead is getting started. The secret of getting started is breaking your complex, overwhelming tasks into small, manageable tasks and then starting on the first one."

— Mark Twain

ACTION IS THE KEY TO SUCCESS

To achieve the next level of success, you must take consistent and massive action. This chapter is about transforming great ideas into reality. So many people have great ideas, but most of them are not acted upon. There are talkers and there are doers. The doers make it happen. As Michael Jordan said, **"Some want it to happen, some wish it would happen, others make it happen."** Be sure YOU make it happen.

Don't get lost in wishful thinking. Success is not about being lucky. To achieve "the habit of success" you need to focus on the most important tasks and succeed in each small task of every day. If you do, you will have a successful week, month, year and lifetime.

Any time you start something new it's easy to become overwhelmed. Wanting something is unfortunately not enough, you must be willing to take action and get busy. It is easy to make a plan, but if you don't step out and do it, it doesn't get done. A lot of people say knowledge is power. I say knowledge is nothing without action.

Give yourself a clear intention and take action. Action always speaks louder than words. Review your Power Goal right now, and make sure it is crystal clear in your mind. Stay committed to this Power Goal, but stay flexible in your approach and your actions. Just do today's work as best you can. A year from now you will be glad you did.

THE RIGHT MOMENT TO START?

"Don't wait. The time will never be just right."

—Napoleon Hill

Don't wait for the right moment. The right moment will never appear. You need to create the right moment and the right moment is here and now.

Excuses For Not Getting Started...

Where you are today has nothing to do with where you are going.

While getting started on this journey, there might be many "ghosts" standing in your way. What will stop you from getting started?

- "I am so far away from the job I really want..."
- "I do not belong to them..."
- "I am not from the right social background..."
- "I don't have enough money to even think about a new way of living..."
- "I don't deserve ..."
- "I will never find a new partner in life...."
- "I don't have enough resources..."

These are the excuses from people with a victim mentality. As Tony Robbins points out, **"It is not about your resources. It's about being resourceful."**

You cannot make somebody else do your pushups, your exercise, meditations, studying, learning a new language, setting Power Goals, practicing new skills or running a marathon. You have to do it yourself, to get any value from it. The last letters in satisfaction are action. Action gives satisfaction!

Stop talking about what you should do and start doing it! It is time to stop waiting for: perfection, inspiration, permission, reassurance, someone to change, the right people to come along, the kids to leave home, a clear set of instructions or a new job.

"The biggest handicap to success is not lack of brains, character or willingness. It is weakness in getting things done."

— Bob Proctor

Do you have a tendency to make up excuses or find "new" and more urgent matters to attend to, instead of actually doing what you should be doing? I know I do every so often. It is not that I don't do things, but I don't do what I am supposed to do. Instead of keeping my Power Goal in focus at all times and concentrating on getting to where I want to be, many times I take detours and make excuses for myself so that I don't feel so bad when I am concentrating on the "wrong" things. A perfect example is when, at work, I start with a "new" project instead of making the 100 calls that will actually bring in the customers. Or when I start doing something around the house and all of a sudden it is too late to go to the gym before picking up the kids, even though one of my Power Goals is about health and staying fit. Giving myself an excuse not to exercise will not make me achieve my Power Goal.

A lot of people are waiting for permission from others. My profession as a Power Goals coach has given me the opportunity to meet with a lot of people who want to rejuvenate their life by taking a new path in life. Many hesitate because they do not feel they have the permission to do that. It is one thing to learn something new, learn how to, and another waiting for permission from somebody else or an organization to allow you to get started. Just go ahead and do it!

When you use an excuse for not accomplishing something or not completing a project, you are actually giving power to someone or something outside of yourself. Regardless of what happens today, absolutely refuse to use an excuse to get off the hook. Excuses cripple you. Have faith that everything will work out and you don't have to figure out exactly how it will come together.

TIME IS IMPORTANT

"If you want to make good use of your time, you've got to know what is most important and then give it all you've got."

— Lee Iacocca

We all have the same amount of time. No one gets any more than anyone else. The busiest individuals in the world only have 24 hours in their day, just like somebody who "does nothing." What matters is what you do with your time. Time is your most valuable asset, so don't waste it. To meet your Power Goals you must move the most important things up front and concentrate on them first.

As Bob Proctor says; **"The ability to effectively prioritize the activities of each day means you have to value your time. If you see your life as valuable and meaningful, then you will value your time as well."**

FIRST, PUT YOUR LIFE IN ORDER

"Order and simplification are the first steps toward the mastery of a subject."

—Thomas Mann

Make room for all the new and beautiful that will come into your life. We tend to store tons of things as well as information that we don't need. Clear your clutter so that your energy can be directed towards your Power Goal. Clean your fridge, clean your wardrobes, clean your garage and clean out your emails.

Clearing clutter is symbolic. You have to get your mind in order before you can bring order to your life and business. Clutter around you means your mind is in a chaotic state and then all you can attract into your life is chaos. It's really all about your mind. Order in your mind will bring order to your life and actions.

I remember working with a person who was always really messy. Her desk was chaotic, her clients were in a mess, she could not pay her bills since her clients would not pay her and she was messy with her clothes. Since she was working in my organization I had to tell her to do something about it.

I looked around and said, "Listen, I'm going on a business trip and I will be back in a week. I want you to really clean this place up. I want it so clean that I can eat off of the floor." She said, "I don't have time to do that. I haven't got enough money to pay my bills. I'm not getting it clean, I have to work." I said, "Listen, if you want me to help you one more time then I want this place clean." She said, "What's that got to do with my problems?" I said,

"You see, as you bring order to your outside world, you of course have to bring order to your inside world. And then everything starts to move for you."

When I came back, the office was spotless. She was smiling and laughing telling me about money that was coming in that had been owed to her for a long time. And I said, "Relate it to your clean office. Before you cleaned up your office and your desk, you had to see it clean in your mind. And then the action was to manifest the picture." If you are having problems, take a look around your office, take a look inside your car and check what your clothes closet looks like.

We hold on to old ideas only because we lack faith in our ability to obtain new ideas. Let go of one idea, before you can move yourself into action on the new idea.

One more thing. Getting yourself neat and tidy also sends messages to your brain and your surroundings. If you are well dressed you will impress upon everyone, including yourself that you are successful. It is worth a try, don't you think?

Ask yourself, "How could I bring greater order to my mind?"

FINISH WHAT IS INCOMPLETE

Unfinished business sucks energy out of you. Every time I start with a new client we do not only focus on the Power Goals, but also what might stand in the way for the right energy to flow into the achievement of the Power Goal. All that is incomplete in your life sucks energy out of you. It can be an unclear financial situation, loans that have not been renegotiated, insurance that needs to be looked over, renovations in your house that you have postponed, photos not having been put into the albums, the garage filled with garbage, a dentist appointment that you have been putting off, car maintenance, incomplete projects, phone calls you have been meaning to make or anything else that takes energy away from the "real stuff."

Make a list of all of the stuff that is sucking energy out of you and start checking them off. You will notice a great relief when you work your way down the list. It truly releases positive energy.

Decide if it needs to be done at all, or simply removed from your life. If major renovation is on your list perhaps moving to another house and releasing yourself from the renovations you never get time to do would be better than sticking to your to-do list?

MOVE ON

"You can't have a better tomorrow if you're thinking about yesterday."

— Charles Kettering

Do you spend your time in the "past?" The past is the place where 95% of the people spend 95% of their time. It is so accepted in our culture for old friends to spend hours and hours reminiscing about "the good old days" from way, way back. We waste hours on past events, negativity, and past injustices instead of using that precious time to get on with our lives in an exciting way. Stop looking back on your life and worrying about things which have occurred and which no longer can be changed.

What you want is action. Sometimes action requires

looking back, to get ahead. Just like a company needs to close the books, so do you. Do you have something standing in your way? Is there something that you need to forgive yourself or somebody else for before you can actually go full speed ahead?

Forgiveness is not something we do for others. We do it for ourselves – to get well and move forward. Dwelling on the past sucks energy out of us. Allow yourself to forgive whatever you need to forgive to move on and operate in the present. Use your precious time to get on with your life in an exciting way.

Identify Opportunities

Opportunities are all around us – all the time. When you become goal oriented you become an opportunity seeker and an opportunity magnet. Your attention will be drawn towards things you may normally have missed. When I first started my business, getting a good office space was crucial. I started dreaming of an office in the best location of downtown Stockholm, with a view and a low rent. It seemed pretty impossible, but dreaming was allowed. Shortly afterwards, a person at a private party walked up to me and asked if I knew about somebody who wanted to rent an office, in a great location and with a low rent … I am still in that great office.

Same thing with cars. Have you ever started dreaming of a particular car and all of a sudden you can see them everywhere? They were there before, but all of a sudden they seem to pop out everywhere.

The same will hold true when you head towards your goal. What you focus on will expand. Signs of opportunity will begin to appear. Keep your mind open especially if you are short on ideas. When you become a goal-oriented individual more and more opportunities will present themselves. Many of them will look good and you will soon get to the point where you have more opportunities than you can pursue. You must be selective and choose only the right opportunities. Otherwise, you will run out of time, money, and energy. Chasing just "OK" can lead you away from greatness.

One opportunity that gets overlooked is being really good at your current core business. Brendon Burchard calls this **"to dig deep"**, stick to your core instead of digging a new hole. Make sure you keep focused on your Power Goals in mind at all times.

DO THE "RIGHT" THINGS

**"Doing more of what does not work
won't make it any better."**

— Charles Givens

Staying in our comfort zone forever isn't going to help you grow. If you really want to start moving forward in your life, you need to dive into something new. Whether you learn a new skill, explore a new path, try a whole new way of living...sometimes the only way to find a better you is to stop being the old you!

When you want something you have never had, you have to do something you have never done. Ask yourself if what you are doing today is getting you closer to where you want to be tomorrow. Face what is not working. Successful people are brave enough to look at what is not going well and take appropriate action, no matter how uncomfortable or challenging it might be. Or else you will just continue doing what is not working and you will just get more of that. Check what is not working by asking: "How can I improve the situation?"

Your mantra needs to be "I am always in the right place at the right time, doing the right things in the right order and I love and respect myself." This automatically makes it happen. I always know and feel that I do the "right" things in the right order. So what is the "right" thing? It is every step and every action.

Program yourself to take the "right" action – doing the things that move you toward your goals, instead of away from it.

FIND OUT WHAT SUCCESSFUL PEOPLE DO

"We tend to minimize the things we can do, the goals we can reach, and yet, for some equally strange reason, we think others can do things we cannot."

— Earl Nightingale

Before moving into brainstorming, a good step is to find out what other people have done. Success leaves trails. You might feel that you are the first person in the world who has ever set such a high-powered goal, but most likely there is someone else who has already achieved what you are seeking to do. Find that person; take their course, read their book, attend their seminar, take them to lunch. What books did they read? What classes did they attend?

Networking is also a great way to gather knowledge.

Attend as many networking events as possible that apply to your Power Goal. Don't just go to any networking event available, but go to the ones that will lead you to your goal. Make sure to have your business cards with you and talk to as many people as possible.

Like Anthony Robbins points out **"find what successful people do, think about and act on and do the same thing."** Surround yourself with experienced people and tap into their wisdom and information.

PREPARE FOR ACTION

"Take a big job and break it into small parts."

—Henry Ford

"The time you want the map ... is before you enter the woods." The lesson is basic: Before you embark on any journey, know in advance how to get where you want to go.

Otherwise, you start doing something and then end up all lost and confused with wasted energy.

Achieving any big goal is a series of small goals. The best way to eat an elephant is one bite at a time. Once you have decided on reaching your big dream, you will have to break it down into smaller goals and then break it down to your weekly and daily activities.

Concrete steps of action will make the difference to you. Goal achievers are in action every day before the masses even start to get ready for their day. Goal achievers make daily commitments and keep them.

You will need to create a written plan of action. Every product or mission has a plan behind it. Every goal-achieving journey is a series of activities that are accomplished in order. A purposeful plan of action is a written "order of activities."

Steps to be followed: If the plan is poorly written or executed, chances are it will fail. I always say, **"if you fail to plan well – well, you plan to fail."**

I always start with the end goal in mind and then back out my timeline from the end to the beginning. I have to do lists that are spread out in columns where I can categorize my activities based on the timing for their completion. Think about your projects the way you would plan a wedding. You have to work backwards from the "date." My to-do lists are broken down into what I have to do over specific periods of time. Start with the end and work backwards.

When I start working with a new coaching client, I first find out what they know about coaching, how they define coaching, then what they expect from their coaching and finally I help them create a plan with 9 steps, the Power Goal Process, and break it down by months, weeks, and days. It's now time to start planning your action.

The step-by-step action process:

- Brainstorm what activities you need to do to get you closer to your defined Power Goal. Make a list of all activities. Don't be too shy to get help from others.
- Prioritize your activities; start with the most urgent tasks.
- Activity plan; take your prioritized list of activities and break it down into an activity plan. Make it specific with time estimations.

- Plan your day in advance. Use your activity plan so that you can easily identify your daily activities. Preferably, plan more than one day ahead.
- Make priorities and always make sure to start with what is most urgent, even though at times it is easier to start with what we know and what is easier to do.

BRAINSTORMING

To find out what action steps need to be taken, brainstorming is a great way to start. Ask yourself; what can I do to reach my Power Goal? Who can I talk to? Who can help me? What are my personal strengths? This is the time to throw as many balls up in the air as possible. It's up to you how to brainstorm. You can do it with others or you can do it by yourself. Don't be too shy to seek help. The more input, the better. But pay attention that the people you brainstorm with are open to change or else the input you get won't be conducive to where you want to go.

Preferably, brainstorming is done with help from your accountability partner, your Mastermind group, your coach, your spouse, your business partner or anybody else who will contribute to you your Power Goals and listing as many actions as possible.

Do you remember when you were little and you could play with the thought of a new game, building a castle or getting married to a prince? Brainstorming is a lot like fantasizing. Open your mind and let yourself freely explore all the different possibilities on how to get to where you want to be. Don't judge what comes out, just let it flow. Be brave, be open. Don't put a lid on yourself. Will you need the help of others, books, courses, trainings, a coaching program or anything else that you haven't even thought of right now? That is why it is valuable to get help from others in this process.

- **Focus on quantity:** The assumption is that the greater the number of ideas generated, the greater the chance of producing a radical and effective solution.
- **Withhold criticism:** In brainstorming don't criticize any ideas. By suspending judgment, participants will feel free to generate unusual ideas.
- **Welcome unusual ideas:** To get a good and long list of ideas, unusual ideas are welcomed. They can be generated by looking at new perspectives and suspending assumptions. These new ways of thinking may provide better solutions. The most successful ideas are usually the most controversial and "different" ones. Thinking outside of the box is value added.
- **Combine and improve ideas:** Good ideas may be combined to form a single better good idea, as suggested by the slogan "1+1=3."

Brainstorming for Right Brains

Right brained thinkers are typically comfortable with a variety of shapes, ideas, and patterns. Right brains don't run from chaos. The artistic side of the right brain enjoys the process of creating, and it doesn't really matter whether they start with cluttered ideas or clumps of clay. The right brain may be most comfortable with mind mapping.

To create a mind map, you will need a few clean pieces of paper, post-its in different colors, some tape, and a few colored pens or highlighters. Or you can use one of the many freeware applications that you can download from the internet.

- Write your main idea or topic in the middle of the paper.
- Start writing down thoughts in no particular order. Write words or passages that pertain to your main idea in some way.
- Once you've exhausted the random thoughts that come into your head, start using prompters like who, what, where, when, and why. Do any of these prompters generate more words and ideas?
- Consider whether prompters like "opposites" or "comparisons" would be relevant to your topic.
- Don't worry about repeating yourself. Just keep writing!
- If your paper gets full, use a second sheet. Tape it to the edge of your original paper.
- Keep attaching pages as necessary.
- Once you have emptied your brain, take a short break from your work.
- When you return with a fresh and rested mind, glance over your work to see what kinds of patterns emerge.
- You'll notice that some thoughts are related to others and some thoughts are repeated.
- Draw yellow circles around the thoughts that are related. The "yellow" ideas will become a subtopic.

- Draw blue circles around other related ideas for another subtopic. Continue this pattern.
- Don't worry if one subtopic has ten circles and another has two.
- Once you finish drawing circles, you may want to number your individual colored circles in some sequence.

You can now turn your wonderful, messy, chaotic creation into a well-organized list of activities.

Brainstorming for "Left Brains"

If the process above makes you break out into a cold sweat, you may be a left brain. If you aren't comfortable with chaos and you need to find a more orderly way to brainstorm, the bullet method might work better for you.

- Put the title or topic of your paper at the head of your paper.
- Think of three or more categories that would serve as subtopics. You can start by thinking of how you could best break down your topic into smaller sections. What sort of features could you use to divide it? You could consider time periods, ingredients, or sections of your subject matter.
- Write down each of your subtopics, leaving a few inches of space between each item.
- Make bullets under each subtopic. If you find you need more space than you've provided under each category, you can transfer your subtopic to a new sheet of paper.
- Don't worry about the order of your subjects as

you write; you will put them into order once you have exhausted all of your ideas.

- Once you have emptied your brain, take a short break from your work.
- When you return with a fresh and rested mind, glance over your work to see what kinds of patterns emerge.
- Number your main ideas so they create a flow of information.
- You have a rough outline for your well-organized list of activities.

After your brainstorming is completed you have a vast list of possible actions, but most probably you will need to gather some more specific information in order to prioritize your actions. The information is out there and that information is easier than ever to access.

You can develop specific information, specific skills or specialized knowledge through books, tapes, courses, trainings, seminars, workshops, internships, searching on the internet, YouTube, volunteering, degrees, certifications, coaching, preparation, practice, rehearsal, etc.

If you have a business related Power Goal, market research is also important. It is not at all necessary to view people or companies that are in the same area as you as competitors. We are all complements to each other. But it is good to get an overview of who is out there, what they sell, what profile they have, and their products and arguments.

As an example, when I decided to write a book I brainstormed with a person who had already written several books. We created a high-level list of activities and among those activities were the following; I had to define a topic, make a complete outline, block time to write, find a publisher, find an editor, find a graphic designer, create a website, take photos, hire a cover designer, complete the manuscript, set a date for publishing the book, find out about promotion, and set a date for the book release party.

Once you a have your vast list of activities, it is time to prioritize.

Prioritize

From brainstorming, you now have your huge list of activities. Can you do all of those things at once?

Of course not. Out of your list you need to evaluate what activities are valid for your Power Goal. Then you need to prioritize the activities.

There are three factors to be taken into consideration:

- How critical is the activity to achieve your Power Goal?
- In what order should the activities be executed?
- And are there any "low-hanging fruits" activities that will easily generate quick results?

Action Plan

"The secret to getting ahead, is getting started."

— Mark Twain

Place your Power Goal at the end of its timeline and then start working backwards. Take your prioritized list of activities and break it down into an activity plan. Make it specific with time estimations. Think about your Power Goal as a project, the way you would plan a wedding. You have to work backwards from the "date." That way you can see what you need to do over specific periods of time. Now it's time to plan the activities in order, or so called time management.

Time management involves putting the important primary activities on a calendar and then being disciplined to perform those activities at the appointed time. It is crucial to goal achievement. Focused time management will accelerate you into your preferred future. It helps you stay on target and keeps you accountable to your schedule. To time manage effectively, you need a weekly calendar and you "block hours" of time to do certain activities. You do this ahead of time so you can keep your weekly activities on track.

Some rules about time management:

- Time Block your personal, and family time first.
- Time Block your weekly primary income producing activities and guard those times ruthlessly.
- Set your calendar and others will accommodate their time to your calendar instead of the other way around.
- Learn how to politely, yet firmly, say "no" to activities that will take you off track. If you say "yes", you say "no" to your own prioritized activities.
- If an unexpected event causes you to miss a primary activity, you must immediately find another time on your calendar to replace the time you missed.

Book a business meeting with yourself to make your priority list and stick to your meeting just like you would with somebody else. That is true prioritizing.

What will have to happen at each phase of the way over time? By doing this you will get a priority list of the things you will have to work on for the week, the month, the quarter and the year. You will find great satisfaction as you cross off your smaller accomplishments along the way. Your list will be rewritten time and time again as you get closer to your deadline. Leonard Bernstein, the great conductor said, **"There are two things you need if you want to accomplish something: a plan, and not quite enough time."**

PLAN EVERY DAY

"Inaction breeds doubt and fear. Action breeds confidence and courage. If you want to conquer fear, do not sit home and think about it. Go out and get busy."

— Dale Carnegie

Make a plan for every day, even the days you plan to have free. This should not take more than 5 minutes per day, but you need to have it in mind for it to happen. Write a map for every day, always with your Power Goal in sight. It is good to plan for the next day on the evening before. That way you are ready to go as soon as you get out of bed. Write down clear, concise actions that will put you on the path towards reaching your goal.

What will you have to add to your daily routine and

what will you have to cut out of your routine to help you to achieve your Power Goal?

I used to run around each day with a list of things in my head of what I needed to do. I had no start, no middle, and no end. There was no structure and most importantly....no order. Then I started to plan out my day the night before. I had a prioritized list from which to work. Goal achieving activities at the top and everything else in order of importance came after with an A, B or C alongside them. This list is now carried around with me every day. I will strike off each task as it is done, not moving onto the subsequent one until the previous one is complete. This creates discipline. Discipline combined with desire and persistence will have you achieving great results.

Jack Canfield practices the "5-rule." It simply means that every day, you do five things that move you towards your goal. It does not happen overnight, but with sustained effort, one action at a time, thousands of individual activities add up to a large success. The "5-rule" is what got Jack and Mark Victor Hanson to become best-selling authors, selling over 50 million copies in 47 languages.

Stay focused all day on what you want to accomplish today. Don't let anybody knock you off track. When you develop a focused mind, you become powerful.

Make up your mind that you are going to do what has to be done today - whether you like it or not - and you will like yourself better at the end of the day.

Set A Deadline

**"One day you will wake up and there
won't be any more time to do the things
you've always wanted. Do it NOW!"**

— Paulo Coelho

Give yourself a deadline on everything you do. Our subconscious works very well to meet deadlines. It is easy to put off important things and trade our time for unnecessary activities. It's easy to be busy and yet not effective. You must consciously move away from being busy to becoming effective. Constantly ask yourself, "Is this what I should be doing right now? What is the most effective use of my time right now?"

Deadlines are productivity motivators. How much do you get done the few days prior to leaving on vacation? Did you ever study really hard that last night before an exam? Thank yourself for having set a deadline.

Begin At Once

**"Create a definite plan for carrying out your
desire and begin at once, whether you're
ready or not, to put this plan into action."**

— Napoleon Hill

Take the first step...
You have got to have a plan and you have to move on it right away - whether you are ready or not. The risk is that the planning becomes an excuse for not setting your plan into action. The Quakers have a good saying, "Pray and

move your feet." A lot of people are always getting ready
to get set to get going. They get a book and they are going
to read it. They have something to do and they are going
to start. But they never do. You see the difference between
the people that make it or not; they move into action.

**"Start where you are, use what you
have and do what you can."**

— Arthur Ashe

Many times I get the question "So, Christina, where and
when do I begin?" Exactly here and now. Exactly where
you are. Even if you are not ready, start anyway. A year
from now you will be really happy you did start now.

Put the plan into action...get going, get busy. It does
not matter if you are ready or not – you still have to start
working towards your Power Goal. Ask yourself: What
can I do today to get closer to my destination?

In *The Habit of Success*, Earl Nightingale says; **"Do
each day all that can be done that day. You don't need
to overwork or to rush blindly into your work trying
to do the greatest possible number of things in the
shortest possible time. It is the quality that counts... the
efficiency of each separate action."** To achieve the "habit
of success," you need only to focus on the most important
tasks and succeed in each small task of each day. If you
have enough of these, you will have a successful week,
month, year and lifetime. Success is not a matter of luck. It
can be predicted and guaranteed, and anyone can achieve
it by following this plan.

No matter how slow your process is or how many
mistakes you make, you are still ahead of those that are

not even trying. Enjoy the easy days and shake off the bad days. Stay steadily on your track. Concentrate on each task of the day and do each as successfully as you can. Take the first step. Do not wait for an opportunity to be all that you want it to be. Step up, move, and keep moving in the direction of your Power Goals. If your goal is to write a book, go home and write the first line, the first sentence. If your Power Goal is to live a healthier life, start by enrolling at a gym and attend your first workout class or set a date with a personal trainer or find any other healthy way to exercise that you love. If your goal is to find your dream home, start by looking at ads or magazines; your first step is to dream what it will be like to live in that house. There is something very powerful about taking that first action. It's like turning the ignition in your car. You will go nowhere until that first simple turn of the key and you start your car.

Now is better than later. **Now** has power. **Now** creates momentum.

Be Prepared To Work Hard

"The biggest handicap to success is not lack of brains, character or willingness. It is weakness in getting things done."

— Bob Proctor

Don't sit and look at a big job and think that it is too big or out of reach. You have to be willing to work hard to reach your goal. How ambitious are you in reaching your Power Goal? Ambition is the expression of your desire. It is the thing that drives you. This is what Napoleon Hill refers to as "what you are willing to sacrifice." It is impossible to achieve something for nothing.

Many seem to believe that just by setting a goal, it will automatically come to you. You cannot just sit around and wait for it. You have to work for it. I just read an article with Steve Blank in Silicon Valley. He says that people tend to believe that people are smarter in Silicon Valley, but it is rather that they work so much harder than the average person. Even though the impression might be that they have a cool lifestyle, working from a café rather than from an office, they tend to work many more long hours with an intense focus on their goals.

You have to get busy. Get a lot of things moving. It is easy to get caught up in the plan, in the philosophy, in the strategy or in the tactics, but if we don't step out and do it, it doesn't get done. Little things really make a difference. Stop talking about what you want to do and start doing it!

"Some people dream of success, while others wake up and work hard at it."

—Winston Churchill

Another impressive person I know is Laslo Szombatfalvy who was born in Budapest, Hungary in 1927, fled to Sweden in 1956 and with no formal education has become the world's third best investor, with 30% return on investment during 46 years in a row. Laslo's achievement is even better than Warren Buffet who has managed to get "only" 20% during 47 years. Laslo's summary of his achievement is "blood, sweat and tears," working every moment of the day on reading about companies, management, investments, and long-term goals. Laslo also continuously worked on educating himself. He would not have made such an impressive result had he not worked so hard.

I can relate to this myself. I have always been hardworking and it has paid off. Ever since I got my first job at H&M after school and during holidays at the age of 15, I have been working hard in everything I do. It is easy to look at people from the outside and think that they did not have to work for where they are today. That is not true. It does not matter where you started from, you always have to work hard to get to where you want to be. Working hard in school, years of travelling around the world with different jobs, years of staying up nights reading and studying, years of learning by attending seminars, and during this time running into many obstacles and tough situations are what helped me reach my goals.

Success requires action and a strong work ethic, not a passive attitude.

COMMITMENT

"People who are interested in doing something will do it when it's convenient; people who are committed will do it no matter what."

— Bob Proctor

Goal achievement is not free. You must commit up front to pay the full price it will take to get you to your dream. There are plenty of unsuccessful people who desire a goal and even decide it is what they want, but never commit to it. Goals without commitment have no power.

Commitment is deciding that the price is worth paying for the goal that will be achieved. Commitment is binding.

You may desire a goal and you may decide that you will go for it, but what seals it is when you commit to it. To commit is "to carry into action deliberately" and "to obligate."

The winners are the ones who decide to commit to themselves and stick to what they commit to.

You have the ability to master anything you do; to become the best at it. People master a certain activity because they decide to and then work at it.

I had a client whose company always seemed to run into problems and challenges. He told me about many occasions when his company was "up against the wall" nearly to the point of bankruptcy. But, because of his and his partners' commitment, they were able to pull through the tough times and eventually made a fortune.

Commitment means there is no alternative but to succeed at accomplishing your goal. The best example of commitment I can think of is parenthood. I would never give up on my kids whatever happens. You must commit to achieving your goal even though there will always be distractions, objections and conflicts that will try to push you off the path. You must give your goal the respect that you would a close family member. In fact, I have heard many times people talk about their dream as their "baby." Writing this book has felt like having a baby. It was exciting to find out that I was "pregnant" as I decided to write the book. At first I kept quiet about it since the first weeks are the most crucial. Then I became so excited that I started telling everyone about the "baby." The closer I got to 9 months, the more there was to carry, the more exciting it was getting, but, also scarier since I had no idea how the delivery would be. Finally, there was the happy delivery and celebration. **"Commit then never quit."**

SELF-DISCIPLINE

"Give yourself a command and then follow it."

—Napoleon Hill

Self-discipline can be defined as the ability to motivate oneself in spite of a negative emotional state. Self-discipline is absolutely essential if you are going to really make things happen in your life. Self-discipline is the bridge between setting goals and achieving goals. No matter how small and unimportant the task may seem, if we do it well, it may soon become the step that will lead us to better things.

Self-discipline for me is to wake up very early, every morning. To be able to do this I had to sacrifice some things. My sacrifice has been not sleeping in, going to bed earlier the night before, not watching TV, etc. I get more things done in the first 4 hours of my day than at any other time during the day. By 9am I have already done my exercises, meditated, called overseas, written my book for an hour, prepared breakfast and taken the kids to school. I am not saying this to sound like a "super-mom" or a "super-woman." It is just that my early activities are now a habit and waking up early is no longer a challenge to me. I realize that I have become much more efficient by doing that and the benefits that I receive from it are huge.

PERSISTENCE

**"Patience, persistence and perspiration
make an unbeatable combination. With
persistence will come success."**

— Napoleon Hill

Do not give up! Keep on going, keep on practicing, keep on doing in order to get to your Power Goal.

To stay with your Power Goal and to stay focused on your action plan, persistence is of outmost importance. Your SUCCESS in anything depends on you knowing how long it takes to succeed - or in sticking with it until you find out. You will win if you don't quit!

Persistence builds character and confidence. It prepares us to push through the resistance during the tough times. It builds our strength to accomplish even greater goals in the future. The greater the goal, the greater the need for persistence. The root of the word persistence means, "stand firm." If your goal is worthwhile enough, you must make a stand for the cause. Too many quit when the going gets tough.

You must have a "never give up" attitude. You must press on towards the accomplishment. It does take work and it does take persistence. There will be times of struggle and times of breakthrough. One thing is for sure; you can't win unless you stay in the game. Yes, it may take longer and take more sweat than you originally signed up for, but if you persist and persevere you will make it to the finish line.

Don't be discouraged if you have days when "it does not work," or if you find that you've reached a plateau.

Plateaus are experienced occasionally in the learning process and you may experience a negative swing, which is part of the natural rhythm process of your life.

Persistence is the key when you feel that you are going backwards. Continue to hold the picture of your Power Goal and your personal success and understand that what is happening to you is preparing you for the good you desire.

Napoleon Hill devoted a lifetime to figure out the reason why certain people succeed. In his book, *Think and Grow Rich,* Hill concluded that persistence is the only thing that separates successful people like Thomas Edison or Henry Ford from the rest of the people in the world.

Persistence is a great quality. It always pays. As Calvin Coolidge said, **"Nothing in the world can take the place of persistence. Talent will not; nothing is more common than unsuccessful people with talent. Genius will not and education will not. Persistence and determination alone are omnipotent."**

When I went to train with Bob Proctor for a full week, he stressed the concept of persistence and suggested that we would read Napoleon Hill's chapter on persistence for 30 days in a row, again being persistent. My accountability partner Jill and I did the exercise for 30 days and it has definitely benefited both of us. You should try it, since staying persistent is tough.

Last year, I met a young girl named Ina at a seminar and we exchanged cards. I did not think much about it, but soon after she called me and wanted to meet. I was very busy and had a hard time fitting it into my calendar. Also, I did not see the purpose in meeting with her, but she was persistent and did not give up. She kept on calling me and said it was rather important to meet with me in person. When she did not give up, I agreed to meet with her and she asked me for advice because her goal is to become a world known rock star. Since she has both the talent and the persistence to not give up her dream, but no money I agreed to work with her pro bono. Despite the fact it is a tough career to pursue, to be a rock star, I became so fascinated with Ina's Power Goal and her persistence. With a little help from me as her coach, with her positive attitude and hard work I will be happy to report on her success which I am convinced will be there sooner than later.

"Persistence during tough periods will be required, but it will be worth the effort."

— Bob Proctor

There are four steps that lead to the habit of persistence:

- Define a purpose backed by a burning desire to attain your goal;
- A plan that is expressed in continuous action;
- A mind closed tightly against all negative and discouraging influences including negative suggestions from relatives, friends and acquaintances;
- A friendly alliance with one or more persons who will encourage you to follow through with your plan and purpose.

If you've never felt the joy of attaining success or

reaching your goal, that should be reason enough to persist. Accomplishment is a wondrous feeling.

"Never give up. Never ever give up. Why? Because just when you are about to give up is when things are about to turn around in a grand way. Hold on. Great things are waiting for you around the corner."

— Sonia Ricotti

There are many great stories on the power of persistence. A rock band was turned down by a major recording company, whose executives scornfully said, "We don't like their sound and besides, guitar music is on the way out." What did the young, struggling Beatles say to themselves when "experts" criticized them? They did not give up.

A fifteen-year-old boy was cut from his high school varsity sophomore basketball team. Despondent, he went home, locked himself in his room and cried. You've heard of him: super star basketball player Michael Jordan, who certainly kept working at his basketball skills, and who said, "I've failed over and over in my life. That's why I succeed."

A young man was fired from his newspaper job. His bosses told him that he "lacked imagination and had no original ideas." Later on the young man had a crazy, never-before-attempted entertainment idea and took his business proposal to over fifty banks. He was turned down by all but the last bank. That young man was Walt Disney.

A young entrepreneur created a new technology called Kazaa to share music and video, but was turned down and sued by both the movie and music industry.

He did not give up. He was convinced that the technology enabled computers to be used as telephones. Niklas Zennstrom was again turned down by investors, but was persistent and created Skype which today has replaced one third of all telephone calls in the world. Napoleon Hill, the great motivational teacher and writer, who made a careful study of how successful people think, said, "Most great people have achieved their greatest success just one step beyond their greatest failure."

Remember that in the confrontation between the stream and the rock, the stream always wins... Not through strength, but through persistence.

BE PRESENT

"Good actions give strength to ourselves and inspire good actions in others."

— Plato (427 BC – 348 BC)

Finally, something that will always payoff is to be present and engaged in everything you do. Be fully here and now. Your presence and engagement will influence all people around you. Every single day you influence people, so make sure you do it well. I'm not telling you it is going to be easy. I'm telling you it's going to be worth it.

ENJOY THE JOURNEY

So many great people throughout history have testified how important it is to enjoy the way to the goal. Michael Josephson said **"Take pride in how far you've come.**

Have faith in how far you can go. But don't forget to enjoy the journey." Something I have been told since I was a young girl are the true words by Karin Boye, "**Yes, there is purpose and meaning in our journey - but it's the way that is worthwhile.**"

Action creates turbulence, terror barriers, excuses and negativity, which cause fear, worry and doubt. Expect it, but welcome it.... to overcome the turbulence you need to go through it - head on!!!

7
EXPECT TURBULENCE

"When we least expect it, life sets us a challenge to test our courage and willingness to change; at such a moment, there is no point in pretending that nothing has happened or in saying that we are not ready. The challenge will not wait. Life does not look back. A week is more than enough time for us to decide whether or not to accept our destiny."

—Paulo Coelho

EXPECT TURBULENCE

When you start to change, you can be sure that both internal turbulence and external turbulence will begin and there will be setbacks.

Your environment which is made up of your family, friends, neighbors, colleagues, etc. will start to react against you doing something new and exciting. Even you will be doubting yourself and questioning your change even though you have a clear picture of what you want to achieve.

Most probably, you will experience internal barriers or "terror barriers," that will delay you achieving your Power Goals. It is natural in the achievement of any goal to come upon obstacles and to feel like you are on a plateau where nothing is moving. Anyone who has ever played a musical instrument, learned a new language or started a new sport knows that you hit plateaus when it seems like you are making NO progress whatsoever. Hang in there. Do not drop out or give up. Doubts, fears, pessimism, and negative thinking poison everything. It is much better to know about it and "welcome" it when it appears, so that you can get yourself into a positive state again.

Without struggle, the butterfly will never fly. You see, a butterfly's struggle to push its way through the tiny opening of a cocoon forces the fluid out of its body and into its wings. No struggle, no flying. Just like the fragile butterfly, the strength you gain in times of trouble will propel you to fly in the future.

Even though there may be roadblocks on your journey, the only real obstacle is what you believe, think and feel about yourself. Remember, there are no limitations. You can be or do anything, if you are clear with what you really want.

Energy and attitude liabilities have no place in your life. These are fear, hopelessness, pessimism, negativity, ignorance, perfectionism, gossip, judgment, hero complexes (I can do it all...) and rescue compulsion (I can save the whole world...).

There are no mistakes – there are only circumstances from which to learn. To choose one's attitude in any given set of circumstances is to choose one's own way.

Your attitude, which includes your thoughts, feelings, and actions, is something you have complete control over today. Do not give yourself any negative energy because there are enough people around you who will probably give it to you anyway. We see the genius in other people, but not in ourselves. We get an idea: "Well, nobody will... that won't work..." That deals with our self-esteem, and our self-image.

Michael Beckwith says: **"When anything 'bad' happens...**

- **It is what it is. Accept it.**
- **Harvest the good.**
- **Forgive all the rest."**

Expect External Turbulence

"You don't have to be the Dalai Lama to tell people that life's about change."

— John Cleese

When you are about to do something different by turning

your intention into action, you will be upsetting the status quo and consequently you may find yourself suddenly creating an array of critics. When you change, your relationship with everything, and everyone, changes too. Change really scares people. Don't let it paralyze you. Simply understand that when you step out of your comfort zone you make other people feel uncomfortable too.

People around you will react to your change. When you decide to start living your dream and making sure you are moving towards your Power Goals, you will run into a major amount of resistance from virtually everyone you know. It is so much more convenient for other people "to have you as you have always been." Fear, envy and jealousy will set in. I am speaking from experience. When I finally took responsibility for my own happiness and decided to divorce, my entire environment of people reacted. My parents did not want me to be different and do something that "nobody in our family had done before." Many of my longtime friends became scared to see our marriage break up, since they thought it was the "perfect marriage." What about their own marriages then? Others were jealous of the fact that I dared to make the decision and go through with it. Many, not so close friends, decided to end our friendship, because of the "fear of contamination." I was no longer invited to the parties that I had previously been invited to…and it hurt. This resulted in fear and doubt of my own. Did I really make the right decision? Is it worth it? Maybe it would just be better to go back "to normal?"

I have another story for you. My daughter recently decided to go to a new school, even though the school she was in is considered the top school in the country. She had been attending that same school for almost 8 years and wanted something different. I felt proud of her daring to question her current situation and make it a Power Goal for herself to change her situation. This is big for a 13-year-old girl and I encouraged her to take full responsibility for her own feelings about the situation and pursue her new dream to be in a different environment. The reaction from the school administration was good, even though such a change was unheard of. But the reaction from some of her so-called friends and their parents was not as pleasant. Even though this had nothing to do with them their reaction was doubt and fear and rejection. Talking bad behind her back was a reaction to her wish to make a change. A dear friend of mine, who is a very experienced psychologist, told me that it can be compared to them being stuck in the "old, small house" and my daughter having rejected her own fears and deciding to go to the castle on the other side of the woods. Now, having reached her "castle," they are still stuck in the "old house."

This is what happens to people around you when you decide to change. They get scared. But you're not supposed to live your life by other people's limitations.

Remember, other people cannot make you feel bad. You allow them to make you feel bad because of what they are saying. As a great person once said, "Don't worry about what others are thinking, it's none of your business!"

NEGATIVE INFLUENCE OF PEOPLE

"Don't be distracted by criticism. The only taste of success some people get is to take a bite out of you."

—Zig Ziglar

Be careful with whom you spend time. Since we are influenced, both positively and negatively, by everyone we spend a great amount of time with, it is important to choose with whom we interact. People around us can be of support or just drag us down. There are times when we have no possibility to influence who we are around, as in school or at work. But there are situations when we can influence those with whom we spend time. Time and energy are our most important assets. It is our own choice to be with people who empower us or with people who suck energy and time out of us. Do you choose who you hang around or do you just spend time with them because it is practical or an old habit? I do not mean that you necessarily need to break with everyone who is not exactly like you, but I would like you to honestly evaluate how you feel when you are around certain people. Do they help you grow? Do you add value to each other's life? Do you have the same values? Does it feel good when you have been in contact, in person or by phone?

Only three percent of the world's population have written goals, this means ninety-seven percent may not share your passion for achievement. It is inevitable that you will get resistance to your new idea or venture from those around you. Just know that it is part of the process. Limit who you talk with about your goal so you prohibit any negative feedback. You need to keep negative, pessimistic people at a distance. A clear sign of negative influence is when people, instead of supporting you, judge you for being brave enough to pursue something new, or they gossip behind your back because you are doing something they do not have the guts to do. Identify the toxic people with whom you need to spend less time. It does not mean you cannot continue being friends, but maybe it would be good for you to spend less time with this person. That will increase the time you have to spend with others or even yourself.

I am a very sociable person and I love being around people, but with age I have come to realize that I need time to myself and I also only want to spend time with people who really inspire me, make me challenge myself and make me grow. I have decided I want to spend as little time as possible with people who are grumpy and complain. I have also decided that negativity in general is not what I want in my life, so I try to cut people out who are negative. Try to figure out which people in your life you really like to be with and who you can "cut out."

If you decide to keep around you the people who empower and energize you, your life will be filled with so much less stress and you will certainly acquire a much better quality of life.

AVOID THE NEGATIVE INFLUENCE OF MEDIA

Negativity of all sorts is not good for your achievement process. Another group to avoid is the news media – newscasters who pour out one bad news story after another. When it comes to the TV, it can often contain more opinions and twisted information than truth since bad news sells better than good news. News can become toxic to your goal achievement intentions. Do not allow yourself to get dragged down by the negativity in the news.

I remember vividly when CNN poured out news on 9/11. Over and over and over again, the plane kept on crashing into the tower and it felt like it was all happening in my living room. Of course that was important news, but what could I do about it except get depressed and negative about the world. This was right around the time when I was going through my divorce and my Power Goal was to take responsibility for myself. When my focus went to the horrible things happening in the world, I was being diverted from my goal. Since then I very selectively watch the news, yet I am still aware of what is going on in the world.

EXPECT INTERNAL TURBULENCE

**"We tend to minimize the things we can do,
the goals we can reach, and yet, for some
equally strange reason, we think others
can do the things that we cannot."**

— Earl Nightingale

Internal turbulence is the feeling that sets in when we do something we have never done before and our comfort zone is being challenged. The truth for many of us is that life can be hard at times, but this is when we have to dig deep and push forward. We have to move away from our comfort zone and create solutions where none seem to exist.

Your new action causes a reaction, and that reaction represents resistance. Resistance is not bad or negative. It is just old paradigms of yours, telling you that you are on a new path. So, the action toward your new Power Goals is what is causing the resistance.

Most of us have limiting perceptions about ourselves that create doubt, fear and limited beliefs about the possibilities to success.

Understand that negative pictures have been put into your mind since you were very young. Maybe you failed a test in school at one time? Your papers were most likely graded with red when you were "wrong." The red marking probably drew your total conscious attention, even if it was the only mark on the entire page. It shifted your energy to the negative and it might have made you fearful of the next mistake you would make. It is this ongoing attention of negativity and failure that keeps people from making any kind of different directional move in their lives, so do not give up! You are on the right track.

CIRCUMSTANCE

"Circumstance may cause interruptions and delays, but never lose sight of your goal. Prepare yourself in every way you can by increasing to your knowledge and adding to your experience, so you can make the most of the opportunity when it occurs."

—Mario Andretti

There are no mistakes – there are only circumstances from which to learn. Have you any idea how many times we let circumstances control us? There are probably circumstances in your life right now of which you are not too fond. Investigate how you can use the circumstance to your benefit instead of letting it rule your life.

I have been deeply touched by Victor Frankl's book, *Man's Search for Meaning,* based on his experiences in concentration camps during World War II. What Frankl found in the camps was that even under the most horrible of conditions, each man or woman had a choice in their reactions. Even though the external conditions were the same, some people reacted as saints, giving their last piece of bread to a dying person, and others as swine, ripping the bread out of the dying person's mouth. He wrote: **"Everything can be taken from a man but one thing: the last of the human freedoms - to choose one's attitude in any given set of circumstances, to choose one's own way."**

As George Bernard Shaw said, **"People are always blaming circumstance for who they are. I do not believe in circumstance. The people who get on in this world are the ones that if they can't find the circumstance they desire they go out and look for the circumstance."**

Do not let the feeling of hopelessness conquer you. Do not tell yourself "There is no way I will be able to achieve something for myself since my circumstances are so small and I have never achieved anything before."

COMFORT ZONE

"Move out of your comfort zone. You can only grow if you are willing to feel awkward and uncomfortable when you try something new."

— Brian Tracy

Moving out of your comfort zone can be really uncomfortable and will undoubtedly create internal turbulence. A Power Goal is a scary goal that is outside of your comfort zone and it will most probably create fear and doubt.

To be in your comfort zone means to be, "Where you feel comfortable, secure and at home." It is a nice feeling to be in there and most people do not want to challenge themselves to leave it, to go and pursue something bigger and better.

But Brian Tracy is right. If you are really comfortable with everything you are doing, you are going sideways - you are not growing.

Be brave. Move out of your comfort zone. Don't be afraid of feeling uncomfortable or awkward. Just step out and make it happen anyway.

JEALOUSY

"To be jealous is to be afraid to lose something you don't have."

— Bob Proctor

What a great definition by Bob Proctor. I often hear people comment or criticize others for how they behave, how they spend their money, for being "over the top" and all it is really, is jealousy.

Have you ever felt that people are jealous of you? It is not a pleasant feeling and it can spoil your efforts towards something new. It creates internal turbulence. When it starts working out for you or you become successful, that is when people around you can get jealous.

I remember when my mother was attacked by jealousy. She was a hardworking, generous person with a great deal of friends and connections. When her career took off she was immediately confronted by jealous people at work who made excuses for her success and criticized how she behaved. It was tough for her to handle and she did not deserve it.

Being jealous of what others have, only reinforces what you don't have and keeps you from having it. Good advice is to not let jealousy rule your life. Don't be jealous of what you don't have, bless those who found a way to get it and find that way yourself.

And, when somebody shows jealousy towards you, maybe it is just your interpretation. Could it be that they are in awe of you, because you are awesome?

FEAR

"Faith and fear have a lot in common, they both demand you believe in something you cannot see..."

— Bob Proctor

Let's discuss indecision, doubt and fear, which are the origin of most everyone's problems. Indecision is the seedling of fear; indecision crystallizes into doubt, and the two blended together become fear... fear being the most crippling.

Fear is a powerful negative emotion. Fear must be erased from the consciousness since it is a great enemy; fear of lacking, fear of failure, fear of sickness, fear of loss and feeling insecurity on some plane. Why are so many people afraid to fail and what are they afraid of? During the process of achieving your Power Goal, fear will appear. What fear will hit you?

- **Fear to step out of your comfort zone** – an attachment to old habits and security, difficulty in leaving the known or "the box." It is so much easier to just stay where you are, but you have to step out of your comfort zone in order to achieve.
- **Fear to fail** – "Even if I try, maybe I will fail. Maybe it is better to not even try." We all fear failure, but we shouldn't. Think of all the famous people who first failed before reaching success. Edison didn't fail...he simply put it as "finding 10,000 ways a light bulb won't work".
- **Fear of poverty** - Many people also experience fear of poverty, which contributes to the lack of persistence. This is today's primal fear that causes you to lose ambition, initiative, imagination, enthusiasm and self-control. Those vital attributes are the core of our existence and the surplus of our success.
- **Fear of the unknown** - building a scenario in your head about what could happen. No facts, only feelings about it. Example: If you walk into the woods, feeling convinced there will be wolves and

bears and you will get lost in the dark... instead of just being inspired by going into the woods, exploring the unknown and looking for the beauty in nature.

- **Fear of being judged by others** - Questions by others like; Is he good enough to do that? Does he have the right qualifications? Why does he believe he is better than us? Who does he think he is? All these questions poison your own judgment.

- **Fear of criticism** - One main cause of fear is "fear of criticism" by others. With the majority of people permitting the public at large to influence them, they cannot live their own lives because they fear criticism. What will others think and say? Will they gossip? Will they talk bad about me? Do they not think I can do this? What will "they" say?

- **Fear of change** - Do I have the guts? Do I dare to be on stage? Am I not serving others enough? Resistance to change can be because you don't feel you have the strength to change.

- **Fear of not being perfect** - Telling yourself that unless it is perfect from the very beginning, it is not worth going for, is another fear. This can cause a new project to never "see the light", a new book never to be released or a new house to never be built ... it's just a bad excuse.

- **Fear of being alone** – If you set a Power Goal that affects your relationship with others, the fear within you can be that people will turn their back on you and not want to associate with you anymore. The fear of being alone is a deep-rooted fear for most of us and it can cause us to freeze instead of moving ahead.

- **Fear of how this new situation, when I have achieved my Power Goal, will it affect my life** – Maybe my friends will leave me? Maybe I will have to divorce? Maybe this will create a new situation at work?

- **Fear of rejection** – Rejection is all in your mind since it does not really exist. If you are in a sales position, asking somebody to buy from you and they say "no", you are really not in a worse position than you were before you asked. So, keep on asking and statistics will tell you that after asking 100 people (or less) you will get a "YES." The same goes if you ask somebody on a date. If they say "no" it is not because you are a horrible person, and you are not in a worse position than before asking. You will have to keep on asking and the right person will say "YES." Do not let rejections stop you from pursuing your Power Goals.

- **Fear of success** – How will I be able to handle it if I become really successful with my new Power Goal? Maybe I am not good enough for this new situation? It might sound ridiculous; however, some people are unable to justify the outcome of being successful in their minds. They become withdrawn and anxious by not being able to comprehend what their lives would look like once they've reached success. Remember, the difference between the person who fails and the one who succeeds is the perception they have. It is seizing an opportunity and acting upon it, unlike the person who allows fear to dominate his abilities.

- **Fear of outshining others** – "I don't dare to be my full self, because it will make others look smaller or not as good."

Victimizing is also part of fear. Feeling sorry for yourself, not being able to do certain things. Telling yourself "I do not deserve better." Who rules that for you? A lot of the time it is only an excuse for the action you should take. Getting scared of what is ahead is not helping you move forward. All this fear and internal turbulence creates anxiety and worry that will be in the way of your success and you will not benefit from it in any respect.

- Do you ever worry beyond reason?
- Does your mind tend to overestimate the risks and underestimate the powers and resources you have to handle those risks?
- Do you feel a subtle, yet persistent, sense of anxiety that runs like an undercurrent beneath your conscious awareness?

Anxiety is the feeling state of fear. Worry is the fretful thinking we do when we feel anxious. Now, a little anxiety and worry can be helpful. Being a bit anxious or worried may inspire you to study for a test, learn a presentation that you have for work, or prepare well for a big event in your life. Anxiety's most productive function is to prepare you for challenges or dangers that you may have to face. For example, if you are preparing for a speech, a little anxiousness may keep you tuned into giving your very best to the audience and paying close attention to what is happening around you. However, anxiety is a problem when it gets triggered often, is overwhelming, or you can't control it. This can cause a chronic state of stress in your body that may lead to difficulty sleeping, exhaustion, irritability, and trouble focusing on what you have to do. It can lead to a downward spiral that is hard to pull yourself out of.

Anxiety can also be a persistent, low-level undercurrent that keeps you from feeling comfortable, confident, happy, and secure in your life. This type of anxiety may be harder to spot, but it is no less important, because it can keep you from living your life to the fullest. When you are anxious and worried you may feel that just getting through the day is achievement enough.

There are two sides to the anxiety and worry equation:

1. Overstating a possible challenge or danger and the likelihood that it will happen.
2. Understating your own abilities and resources to handle that challenge or danger.

In other words, when you feel anxious you are looking at what might happen and seeing it as hugely dangerous and highly likely to happen. At the same time, you are feeling that your talents, skills, and resources are small, inadequate, and not up to the challenge that you face. What you are facing looks like a huge "catastrophe."

A lot of people get Valium and Prozac and other remedies for their anxiety. What they should be dealing with is the cause of the anxiety, which is the fear. And that is an emotional state that is caused by doubt or worry. Let's talk about what you can do about anxiety.

There are ways to work against it.

How To Handle Anxiety

**"Love the things that are in the way
of where we want to get to."**

— Gay Hendricks

Unless you take steps to curb your anxiety and manage your worry, it can take you into a downward spiral that can be difficult to escape. What steps can you take before that happens? And what can you do to pull yourself out of it if it does happen?

Awareness is the first and most essential step to anything you want to change. One great strategy is to keep an 'Anxiety Journal' to record moments of anxiety and worry. It enables you to identify anxiety-worry as soon as it arises, then you can insert a mental pause into your reaction and do something about it. Here's a way to do that:

Whenever you feel anxiety and worry, pause, take a break from what you are doing, practice slow deep breathing to calm yourself, and, then, take a few moments to record the following elements:

- Rate the intensity of your feeling from 0-10 (10 being extremely anxious).
- Make note of what triggered your anxious feeling. What happened right before you felt this way?
- Make note of the worry thoughts that accompany this feeling.
- Make note of any physical symptoms such as muscle tightness, irritability, sweating, trembling, confusion, difficulty sleeping and so on.

- Make note of any worry behaviors such as excessive checking to make sure things are okay, not sleeping at night or extreme compensations such as showing up an hour early for an event. Reality check. Assess how likely it is that what you are worried about will actually happen. What can you do here and now to eliminate the risk of it happening? If it did happen, what could you do about it? What actions could you take? What is a more realistic and helpful way to think about the situation?

- Make sure to get help with all of the above if it feels too challenging or overwhelming to get a grip on it yourself. Remember all the supportive people that you have identified (Chapter 4).

Shining the light of awareness on anxiety in this way helps to quickly dissolve it. After going through that process, you are much more conscious of the dynamics behind your anxiety-worry reaction. You have faced possible outcomes directly and you have imagined what you can do no matter what happens.

You'll likely revise your assessment of what could happen so that you see things less dramatically, less catastrophically. You'll likely revise your sense of your own abilities and resources more favorably. Hopefully you feel up to the challenges you might face. You'll likely feel more confident and empowered.

If you are experiencing fear, understand this, you get rid of fear by facing it. Face the thing you fear and fear will leave you. Absolutely refuse to go through your life or face any situation in a state of fear. Make up your mind right now that you are absolutely going to eliminate fear from your life. Now, that doesn't mean it is not going to come into your mind. It will but, when it does, kick it right out.

There are many other strategies to handle fear and anxiety when it arrives at your doorstep.

"Relax into who you really are."

— Jill Hutchison

- **Cognitive behavior therapy (CBT)** is a type of psychotherapeutic treatment that teaches people how to identify and change destructive or disturbing thought patterns that have a negative influence on behavior. CBT is commonly used to treat a wide range of disorders including addiction, depression and anxiety. CBT is based on the idea that our thoughts cause our feelings and behaviors, not external things, like people, situations, and events. The benefit of this fact is that we can change the way we think to feel and act better even if the situation does not change. CBT is considered among the most rapid in terms of results obtained.

- **Yoga** – There are many different kinds of yoga, but all are related to finding a space for yourself and stilling your mind.

- **Meditation** - the regular practice of meditation will help you clear out distractions. Ask for guidance. Visualize light around you. With palms facing up on your lap, repeat "I am love." After 10-20 minutes start to close down by again visualizing white light surrounding your body. Ask for guidance and protection during the day and see yourself accomplishing your goal for the day. Walking meditation is another way to work with difficult emotions.

- **Mindfulness** – to handle anxiety by breathing in and out peacefully. It is about bringing one's complete attention to the present moment, non-judgmentally.
- **Tapping** – Like acupuncture and acupressure, based on Eastern medicine. Tapping is a set of techniques which utilize the body's energy meridian points. You can stimulate these meridian points by tapping on them with your fingertips – literally tapping into your body's own energy and healing power Go to www.thetappingsolution. com and learn more.
- **The Sedona Method** – The Sedona Method is technique that allows you to uncover you own ability to let the painful or unwanted feelings go – feelings that happen in the moment. It is done by using a series of questions that help you lead yourself to being self-aware of what you are feeling in the moment and gently guide you into the experience of letting go. Go to www.sedona. com and learn more.
- **Hypnosis** - We operate in 4 levels of consciousness; therefore, each scenario will determine what hypnotic level your hypnotherapist will place you in. It is safe and effective. Many people use hypnosis as a way to learn how to relax. In hypnosis, positive affirmations are therapeutically

placed in the subconscious mind to override the current negative thought patterns.

- **NLP** - Neuro Linguistics Programming takes its meaning from these words: Neuro: derived through and from our senses and central nervous system; Linguistics: our mental processes are given meaning, coded, organized, and, then transformed through language; and Programming: how people interact as a system in which experience and communication are composed of sequences of patterns. NLP is the systematic study of human performance that lets you model or copy it in any form. It is a multi-dimensional process that changes behavioral patterns and the tools and techniques are extremely beneficial (especially in children). To learn more about hypnosis and NLP, go to: www.lifecoachingandbeyond.com and click on the tabs at the top that pertain to each.
- **Affirmations** – As spoken about earlier, affirmations are a powerful way to program your subconscious consciously. An example of a great affirmation when in distress and in turbulence: "I am knowledgeable and well organized. My ability is so great I can achieve anything."
- **Creative Imagination**, and finding positivity from looking at your vision board.

When people have fear they don't even take the first step. Get in the game!

DOUBT

"Doubt of whatever kind can be eliminated by action!"

— Thomas Carlyle

Limiting beliefs and negative self-talk are the very source of doubt. Doubt freezes a lot of people. Doubt and worry are both like diseases that some people have turned into habits. Doubt of any kind can be ended by action. Don't sit wondering whether you can do something, "Is it really possible to achieve a Power Goal that big?" Just go and do it! You probably do not feel ready, but once you start, going into action, your doubt will disappear. That is what I did when I started my first company. I was feeling scared and I was doubting if I had done the right thing quitting a daytime job and leaving the corporate world to go into something unknown. I was doubting if I had made the right decision. I doubted if I would succeed. I doubted if I would get any customers. Well, I started doing and soon I realized I was good at what I was doing. Just sitting around will not get any new customers. Action was the key to my success and eliminated the doubt that I could do it.

The "cost" of energy is very high when you are doubting and worrying. Doubt and worry are really contra-productive. Just imagine if I had used all that energy to actually start building my company instead of doubting myself and worrying about the future.

When in doubt, ask yourself "How much do I actually want this?" and "How much am I willing to sacrifice to achieve my Power Goal?" If you have a clear picture of your Power Goal and what you REALLY want, there should be no doubt in your mind. Just do it, because you can do it!!!!

NEGATIVE SELF-TALK

**"If you are going to doubt anything,
doubt your limitations."**

— Bob Proctor

Negative thinking is the very source of poison in your life. Self-doubt, self-criticism, and negative self-talk will ruin a lot for you. Do you talk to yourself, putting yourself down? Research indicates that the average person, you and I, talk to ourselves about 50,000 times a day and most of that talk is about ourselves. According to researchers, it is 80% negative, such as;

- "I am never going to be able to do that."
- "I don't have the right education."
- "I am not good enough."
- "I will not pass that exam."
- "I'm not a good speaker."
- "I know they don't like me."
- "I don't look good today... I never look good."
- "I will never get a raise."
- "I can't find a new job."
- "I don't have the qualifications."
- "I'm always late."
- "I shouldn't have said that."
- "I am so stupid."
- "I have to be perfect to be loved."

- "I need approval to be successful."
- "What if somebody criticizes what I am doing?"
- "Is it worth it?"
- "All this hard work and what will I get out of it?"
- "I can never do anything right."
- "No one listens to me anyway."
- "People will not love me if I change."
- "I am not smart enough."
- "In our family, we do not do that."
- "I am not sure he/ she is the one for me."
- "Is this the right job for me?"
- "It is the right time to release this product or should I wait?"
- "Is this really the right market?"

Think about if you could change all that negative self-talk into positive self-talk. Eighty percent of positive self-talk would equal 40,000 times a day. Do you think that would affect your life and your self-image in a positive way?

Even though I have worked with hundreds of clients guiding them through doubts and negative self-talk, I still get caught in the internal turbulence myself. While writing this book, I woke up at four o'clock in the morning feeling terrible, telling myself that "I will never be able to finish this book, I will never be able to launch it, never be able to stand up and tell people about it and definitely not put my name out in the world and proudly present it." I was horribly upset and decided to call my close friends around the world, since I could not talk to anyone so early in the morning in Sweden. I called my friend Carrie in Canada, then my friend Peggy in the US and finally I called my friend Jill in Australia. They were all wondering why I was putting myself down so much and I could not explain it, it was just there. When my husband woke up he started laughing, telling me that I should start reading my own book. This is all about the old paradigm calling on you. Being out of the comfort-zone is scary, but it is the only way to grow. Self-doubt is not of use to us, so we'd better be aware of it when it sets in. Just keep on going.

These energy and attitude liabilities have no place in your life. They won't help your mindset. They won't help you get to the Power Goal you have set up for yourself to achieve. Eliminating them from your life will bring about a new, more positive, you – filled with more energy and ready to jump on any opportunity that comes your way. Yes! It's time to be excited about yourself and what you can achieve.

WHAT TO DO WHEN THE NEGATIVE SELF TALK SETS IN

Decide before it even happens, what to tell yourself, if negative self-talk sets in. Make a list of things that you have achieved, done well, or have been acknowledged for and this will shift your energy and your focus. Decide to pick yourself up when the negativity sets in.

These are ways to overcome negative beliefs:

1. Identify your negative limiting belief (what I tell myself).
2. Identify how this negative belief limits you.
3. Decide how you would like it to be.

4. Write a turnaround statement and give yourself permission to be the new way you decided on in step 3.
5. Repeat the new statement. This is your affirmation for the next 30 days. Implant it in your subconscious.

Example:

1. My limiting belief is: "I never do anything right."
2. This makes me not want to try doing new things.
3. I want to feel happy and excited doing new things.
4. New statement: "I am so happy and grateful I can do many things right and I love trying new ways of doing it. I learn and get better all the time."
5. Repeat for the next 30 days.

Write down your own limiting beliefs:

1. My limiting belief is _____.
2. This makes me _____.
3. I want to _____.
4. Turnaround statement: "I am so happy and grateful now that _____.
5. Repeat for the next 30 days.

You should be grateful for the scary feeling that tells you that you are out of your comfort-zone, seeing the beauty of growing and appreciating the feeling of gratitude towards yourself that "I am brave enough to not stay in my comfort-zone and taking new steps towards something different, such as my Power Goal."

To be successful, you have to take risks and part of that is your own willingness to reject the negative self-talk.

What exactly is it that you fear? You have already figured out what your Power Goals are, you have already been working towards it for some time and to give up at this point would be like not giving yourself what you deserve. Rethink and write down what it would cost you to give up at this stage.

We are usually the only ones standing in the way of our own success, money, love and happiness. How do we get out of our own way and how do we stay out of our own way? You must give yourself the affirmation of what you want. Act as if you already have it. What is going on inside of you? Be relaxed and let it float to you. See yourself the way you want it to be. It is never outside of you, it is inside of you. See it in your mind and attract the people you have to attract.

WHAT ELSE CAN CAUSE TURBULENCE?

"We simply do not understand our place in the Universe and have not the courage to admit it."

— Barry Lopez

The universe can cause turbulence. How is this, you might wonder? Well, when you have decided on your Power Goal and you are working hard to achieve it, that is when you might get challenged in strange ways.

Once you have your mind set to doing something big, it is like somebody or something will challenge you and ask you if you REALLY want to do it. This challenge can be a positive challenge. Have you ever decided to change your job and then you get offered a better position at the old company?

My husband had just decided to start his own company after years of thoughts and doubt about this. He is a guy who likes security and was feeling very proud that he had finally made the decision. Right after his decision was made, he was offered a great position at an multinational company, as part of the management group. An offer that seemed almost impossible to turn down. Luckily, he was able to stop himself from accepting it and instead stayed with his original decision, to pursue his dream of having his own company. When these challenges that appear to be nothing but positive occur, it is important to say "thanks but no thanks" and let them pass. It is just proof you are on the right track. Never let go of your Power Goal. Do not let anybody steal your dream.

DESPITE ALL THE TURBULENCE, ARE YOU STILL WILLING TO CHANGE?

"Obstacles can't stop you. Problems can't stop you. Most of all, other people can't stop you. Only you can stop you."

— Jeffrey Gitomer

Are you allowing turbulence and setbacks to control you? What type of setbacks are stopping you?

Do you have an excuse for not continuing to reach your Power Goal? How much time do you let a setback take until you are up and running toward your Power Goal again? Are you ready to eliminate the self-sabotage, fear, and uncertainty and actively pursuing the dream that is right for you – the dream that will result in the joy and confidence you crave?

Are you relying on you? When you know that you are capable of dealing with whatever comes, you have the only security life can offer. It is not in what other people think, it is not in a job or anything else on the outside of you. Security is an inside thing. When you know you are capable of dealing with whatever comes, you have the only security the world has to offer.

We all know that if you want to get something different from your life you have to be different.. It isn't enough to act differently; you have to create different beliefs. Willingness is a big missing step, and it needs to be your first step. I know you are excited about transforming your life. I know you want it more than anything, but are you really willing to be different? There is a difference between desire and willingness and you can transform your desire into willingness and then move into action.

Let's counter that discouragement with encouragement; procrastination with persistence; rid yourself of negativity. It's time to bring out that positive attitude.

8
STAY POSITIVE

"There is a basic law that like attracts like.
Negative thinking definitely attracts negative
results. Conversely, if a person habitually thinks
optimistically and hopefully, his positive thinking
sets in motion creative forces. And success,
instead of eluding him, flows toward him."

—Dr. Norman Vincent Peale

POSITIVE OUTLOOK ON LIFE

**"People who accomplish great things
are aware of the negative, but give all of
their mental energy to the positive."**

— Bob Proctor

It is easy to be negative and it takes work to be positive. Successful people maintain a positive focus, no matter what is going on around them. Stay focused on past successes, instead of dwelling on your failures.

Having a positive outlook on life will get you far. Success and feeling bad do not go well together. Success always makes you feel good, and it wakes up something inside that you may not have even known was there. Think of all the successes you've had … pick six or seven of these and remember how you felt. Would you like to feel that way more often than not - or even all the time?

POSITIVE ATTITUDE

"Attitude is the magic word."

— Earl Nightingale

To have a positive outlook on life is the same as operating with a positive attitude. There is really only one thing that you can control and that is your attitude. Attitude is the combination of your thoughts, your feelings and your actions.

To have a positive attitude, you need to focus on the solution and not on the problem. If we have the wrong attitude, it distorts everything that comes into our life.

When we have the right attitude we improve everything around us, we build strong relationships with people who can help us, and our outlook on life is geared towards solutions.

Ricardo Frode, living in Portugal where the economic crisis has hit hard, decided he wanted to show to the Portuguese people that it is possible to do what nobody else believed to be possible. He decided he would set up a really tough project that was close to impossible to succeed with, in order to prove to people that with the right attitude anything can be done. He decided he would go with NO money, NO phone, and NO computer from the very north of Europe to the south of Europe and by that show the people of Portugal that it is possible to do the seemingly impossible as long as you focus on the solution and not on the problem.

He did it! Ricardo travelled from Portugal to as far up North of Scandinavia as he could get. He landed in Skellefteå, Sweden in the middle of the winter, at -30 degrees Celsius (-22 Fahrenheit). Arriving from the south of Europe, this was the first shock to him. Without any money, he managed to get food, shelter, train fares, get on buses, stay with people, hitch hike through Europe and in less than two weeks travel more than 4500 km, without starving.

I hardly knew him, but he rang me up and asked if we could have a coffee together or if he could stay with me. I was surprised and amazed that someone like him could travel with no money and no concrete plans. I know the value of goals and staying focused on the solution, but I was still shocked. He made it possible since he kept his focus on the solution, not on the problem. And he did not feel sorry for himself. How far can you get with the right attitude?

"If we are basically positive in attitude, expecting and envisioning pleasure, satisfaction and happiness, we will attract and create people, situations, and events which conform to our positive expectations. So the more positive energy we put into imaging what we want, the more it begins to manifest in our lives."

— Shakti Gawain

The law of attraction says, "Like attracts like," so when you have a thought, you are also attracting "like" thoughts to yourself. That is why it is so important to be careful about what thoughts you have – positive or negative. Your current thoughts are creating your future life. The beautiful truth about this is when you really get involved in positive thinking, you set up a vibration that causes positive energy to flow to you. You don't even have to look for it, it is just there.

A good attitude, a good concept for success is "to bite off more than you can chew." Don't be afraid to tackle the big jobs. Don't even entertain the thought that you can't! Just think, "I don't know how, but the way will be shown."

Like Norman Vincent Peale said; **"People become really quite remarkable when they start thinking that they can do things. When they believe in themselves they have the first secret of success."**

THE MAGIC OF POSITIVE THINKING

"As we think in our hearts so are we. We are literally what we think, our being is the complete sum of all our thoughts."

— James Allen

The happiness of your life depends upon the quality of your thoughts. We are what we think; therefore if our thoughts are healthy and beneficial, joy will follow us. We are the master of our thoughts, the molder of our character, and the maker of our condition, environment and destiny. You hold the key to every situation and contain within yourself that transforming agency by which you may make yourself what you will. Think only positive thoughts. Positive thoughts open the door to success and happiness. We become what we think about all day long. Our thoughts determine whether we're being empowered or weakened. The most empowering thoughts you can have are those of peace, joy, love, acceptance, gratefulness and willingness.

Just like it is important to feed your computer with the right programs, it is just as important to hold the "right" thoughts and think positively. Remember that your brain can only hold one thought at a time, so the best way to achieve success is to only focus on the positive and not allow the negative to enter into your mind.

Yes, there is magic in positive thinking! In aviation, the word attitude means the angle at which the plane meets the wind, whether the wings are level with the horizon, and whether it is climbing or descending. The pilot who fails to take responsibility for the attitude of his aircraft is in serious trouble. And likewise, any person who has not taken charge of his or her own beliefs and attitudes runs a similar risk.

The key to cultivating and maintaining a positive mental attitude is to take control of your thinking and avoid negative minded people. It's a challenging task to develop a calm, focused mind, but well worth the effort.

I've heard it said countless times that simply thinking positive thoughts isn't enough. Rather than argue that point, I prefer to refer to the wise words of Zig Ziglar who said, **"positive thinking will let you do everything better than negative thinking will."** In other words, even if it only helps a little - those who strive to put positive thinking to work in their lives are better off than those who don't.

Negative thoughts affect your body negatively, by making you uptight, increasing your blood pressure and your breathing rate, giving you tight muscles, and causing you to sweat. Positive thoughts affect you in a positive way, making you more relaxed, centered and alert.

Your current thoughts are creating your future life. **"Life is an echo; what you send out comes back"** is an old Zen proverb. The beautiful truth about this is when you really get involved in positive thinking, you set up a vibration that causes positive energy to flow to you. You don't even have to look for it, it is just there.

"The happiness of your life depends upon the quality of your thoughts..."

—Marcus Aurelius

Positive Words

We live in a world of words. We can be empowered or weakened by words. We program ourselves and others by words. Our words create pictures in our minds. Words such as love, happiness, success, achievement, joy and ability describe conditions all of us want. By speaking these words and words that gear us towards these conditions, our state of mind will make us stay positive.

Conversely, if we do not watch our language and repeat negative words, negative things will come to us. Be aware of what you say! Masaru Emoto is a Japanese author and entrepreneur, best known for his claims that human consciousness has an effect on the molecular structure of water. According to his research, positive words create beautiful crystal formations and horrid words break those crystals down. Since the human body consists of 60 percent water we should be aware of our wording.

Change your self-talk. We all carry on an inner dialogue with ourselves that is often called "self-talk." When this inner conversation is negative, our mood is usually low. Research has shown that we can change our mood by changing the tone of the things we say to ourselves.

Talk to yourself as a winner. Transform all negative self-talk into positive self-talk.

GRATITUDE

"You will know when you have found true gratitude, because you will become a true giver. You give joy, love, money, appreciation, compliments and you give kindness."

— Wallace D. Wattles

Gratitude is a powerful energy and an amazing way out of negativity. Gratitude is a feeling so feel it as much as you can. Be grateful for all the good in your life and this will create miracles in your life. Being grateful for what you have wipes out negativity and brings abundance in all things. BUT gratitude is just a word unless you feel it intensely and deeply. You must practice gratitude regularly to really reach the greatest feeling and the highest frequency in order to harness the power of gratitude.

Being grateful is a choice. It's about learning from a challenging situation and taking the good out of it to help deal with the challenge. It's about realizing you have more power over your life and thoughts, and emotions and energy than you previously imagined. You can stop being a victim of your circumstance and reach out for the joy in living. If you can open your heart to the good all around, gratitude can become as much a part of your life as breathing. Look for the gifts in everything and be grateful. Many people focus on the one thing they want and then forget to be grateful for all the things they already have. When things seem to be tough, those are the biggest lessons and ultimately we grow and learn from everything. Be grateful for the learning and harvest the good.

Living Gratitude Daily

"Be thankful for what you have and you'll end up having more. If you concentrate on what you don't have you will never have enough."

— Oprah Winfrey

To change things quickly, commit to writing 10 things you are grateful for each day, until you see the change. And FEEL the gratitude. Your power is in the feeling that you put into the words of gratitude.

Here are a few helpful suggestions to help you get started on your gratitude practice. Pick the gratitude practice that resonates best with you.

1. **Start every morning by saying "Thank you."**
    The magic formula is:

    *   Recognize the feeling of gratitude for the new day;
    *   Recognize all that you are grateful for in your life and make a list of 10 blessings;
    *   Deliberately say the magic words "Thank you";
    *   The more gratitude you deliberately think and feel, the more positivity you will receive.

2. **Keep a Daily Gratitude Journal.**
    Keeping a gratitude journal is probably the most effective strategy for increasing your level of gratitude. Set aside time, daily, to record several things for which you are grateful. You can write

when you get up or at the end of the day. Pick a time that you will consistently have available. The important thing is to establish the daily practice of paying attention to gratitude-inspiring events and to write them down.

3. **Use Visual Reminders.**

Two obstacles to being grateful are forgetfulness and lack of awareness. You can counter them by giving yourself visual cues that trigger thoughts of gratitude. I like to use post-it notes listing blessings in many places, including on the refrigerator, mirrors and the steering wheel of my car. You can get as creative as you want and you can even use your camera to take photos of what you're grateful for and put them in an album or on your computer screensaver. Another strategy is to set a pager, computer or your cellphone to signal you at random times during the day and to use the alarm as a signal to pause and count blessings.

4. **Have a Gratitude Partner.**

Social support encourages healthy behaviors, because we often lack the discipline to do things on our own. Just as you may be more likely to exercise if you have an exercise partner or participate in a class, you may be able to maintain the discipline of gratitude more easily if you have a partner with whom to share gratitude lists and to discuss the effects of gratitude in your life. If you hang out with ungrateful people, you will "catch" one set of emotions; if you associate with grateful people, you will catch gratefulness. Find a grateful person or community and spend more time with them.

5. **Make a Public Commitment.**

   When we become accountable and we make commitments to others, we are more likely to follow through. Why not post your daily gratitude on Facebook?

6. **Go on a Gratitude Walk.**

   Something about getting out in nature is healing. Research shows exercise can decrease stress and release the "feel good" chemicals in your brain. Giving thanks helps you become centered, present and living in the moment. When you are grateful for the beauty all around, you automatically find more beauty for which to be grateful.

7. **The Magic Gratitude Rock.**

   Use a beautiful rock to remind yourself to be grateful. You can keep it in your pocket, on your desk or on your bedside table which will remind you at a certain time of the day about the things for which you are grateful. I have a plain grey rock with the inscription "TACK" on it. That means "thank you" in Swedish and I always feel very grateful when I see it or hold it.

8. **Self Gratitude.**

   Be thankful to yourself for any accomplishment and be grateful who you are. Every day, look at yourself in the mirror - look yourself in the eyes and say, "I love you... really." This exercise is based on the simple principle that we all need daily acknowledgment and gratitude.

"Gratitude is the single most important ingredient to living a successful and fulfilled life."

— Jack Canfield

Have an attitude of gratitude, including self-gratitude. Start to think of all the things you are grateful for and list them. Acknowledge your successes.

If you feel it is hard to get started with your gratitude practice, here are some examples of what you can be grateful for:

- I am so grateful for my health.
- I am so grateful for my friends.
- I am so grateful for the business that I am in.
- I am so grateful that the sun is shining today.
- I am so grateful my kids are healthy.
- I am so grateful I have food on the table.
- I am so grateful my parents are helping me out.
- I am so grateful I can see.
- I am so grateful I have a job that I like.
- I am so grateful I have a loving husband/wife.
- I am so grateful...

THINK AND THANK

"Celebrate what you want to see more of."

— Tom Peters

It cannot be overlooked that thank and think are only a letter apart. That's because they're related. As far back as the year 1000, there are references in Old English to thank meaning "good thoughts or gratitude." To think, in Old

English, means "to conceive in the mind." I really like the "conceive" part. We know what it means to conceive a baby, and if we study the Latin word for conceive we find it means "to take in and hold." So think thoughts of thanks, let them take hold in your heart. The more you do, the more your actions will reflect those thoughts, and the more thankful actions you take, the more thankful you will ultimately feel. So how good do you want to feel? What thoughts are you going to take in and hold today? Do kind things for others, praise others with secret niceties. Loving actions and loving thoughts will take root and they will blossom by expression through your hands, your voice, your eyes, and through the living of your dreams and your Power Goals.

ACKNOWLEDGE ALL THAT IS WORKING

If you start to see something change for the better, make sure to appreciate and acknowledge that it is happening.

- If you meet with the "right" person, acknowledge it.
- If you find the perfect parking space, because you were thinking and hoping for it, acknowledge and thank for it.
- If you get extra money from an unexpected source, acknowledge it.
- When you get the special table that is always taken at your favorite restaurant, acknowledge it and be grateful that you got it today.
- When someone you did not expect is supporting you in achieving your Power Goal, make sure to appreciate and acknowledge it.

- Be thankful for the food after every meal. This is something we do in Sweden by old tradition and it is not until now that I fully understand the power of saying "Thank you" or "TACK."

COMPLIMENTS

Many of us are unable to receive compliments. We are trained from toddlers to beat ourselves up for the things we do wrong, and not to congratulate the good. We have also been taught to love our neighbor, but nothing has been taught about loving ourselves. It is vitally important that we love ourselves in order to love others unconditionally. Without learning to love yourself, you cannot truly know how to love others. When you do not love yourself, it shows; and all you will attract are others who do not love themselves. There are no successes in that.

Do you have your channels open? Some people call it "the receiving channels." We all have these channels, but because of upbringing and paradigms, many of us keep these channels closed. Check to see if you have your channels open:

- Do you receive compliments well?
- Do you receive unexpected gifts easily?
- Do you accept help when it is offered?
- Do you accept when somebody offers to pay for your meal?

These may seem like little things, but they will help you know if you are open to receiving what you have been wishing for.

So if someone gives you a compliment or compliments something you wear, just receive it and say "thank you."

FEED YOU BRAIN WITH POSITIVE MESSAGES

- Reject negativity such as the news and papers with negative information.
- Nature abhors a vacuum – so fill your time with interesting things such as positive, uplifting motivational videos.
- Affirmations are great tools in reconditioning our thoughts. Here is an example of an affirmation to focus yourself on positivity: "I solve all of my challenges in an easy manner. Solutions come easily to me, and my mind is filled with positive thoughts."
- Watch funny movies.
- Read comic strips.
- Listen to positive talk shows.

BELIEVE IN YOUR POWER GOALS

"You can be anything you want to be, if only you believe with sufficient conviction and act in accordance with your faith, for whatever the mind can conceive and believe, the mind can achieve."

—Napoleon Hill

You get what you expect. Have faith that it will all fall into place, and believe your Power Goals will come true. Do not let anybody take away your dream. When you are firmly grounded in faith, negative thoughts will have no power over you.

> "Imagine with all your mind, believe with all your heart, achieve with all your might."
>
> — Unknown

BELIEVE IN YOURSELF

> "Those who win are those who think they can."
>
> — Richard Bach

Believing in yourself is a choice. It is an attitude you develop over time. It helps if you got positive reinforcement from your parents, but even with limiting beliefs and negative conditioning, it is now your own responsibility to believe in yourself.

It is all about self-value and your abilities. Believe that you can do anything. If you want love and respect, you have to start by appreciating it in yourself. It is only you who can fill up your need for self-respect, despite what others are saying, doing or thinking.

> "Our deepest fear is not that we are inadequate. Our deepest fear is that we are powerful beyond measure. It is our light, not our darkness that most frightens us. We ask ourselves, "Who am I to be brilliant, gorgeous, talented, fabulous?" Actually, who are you not to be? You are a child of God. Your playing small does not serve the world. There is nothing enlightened about shrinking so that other people won't feel insecure around you. We are all meant to shine, as children do. We were born to make manifest

the glory of God that is within us. It's not just in some
of us; it's in everyone. And as we let our own light
shine, we unconsciously give other people permission
to do the same. As we are liberated from our own
fear, our presence automatically liberates others."

— Nelson Mandela

Why do we belittle ourselves? It seems that what scares us
more than anything else is our own greatness. We are all
incredibly powerful. Believing in yourself makes it easier
to strive for what you really want. I realize that until now
I have belittled myself by not daring to be different or
speak up. I have kept myself down in order to not stand
out. I have not told people what I believe in, until now.
Finally, I am convinced that I want to share my views and
my opinions with the world. No more do I want other
people's views of the world to be more important than my
view. I want to acknowledge to myself what I am good at
and I want to be proud of it.

Successful people know what they are good at. Make
sure, you are one of them. Find as much good as you can
in yourself and fill yourself with it. Go for it!

- **Make a victory log** – a written record of your
  successes. This is easier said than done. Give
  yourself permission to note down your successes.
- **Work with a positivity book** – write down
  anything that can get you charged. I have a book
  in which I regularly work on my Power Goals, my
  action plan, affirmations and success list. You can
  also use it to keep a journal of your progress, every
  day or every week.

- **Self-appreciation** – write down everything positive that you would like to say to yourself or you would like others to say to you.
- **Give acknowledgement to yourself, looking into a mirror.**
- **Give good feedback to others** – and it will make you see the greatness in yourself. For example, say this: One thing I specifically appreciate about you is... You can do this with yourself, too, even though it might feel funny to begin with. It is important to appreciate ourselves.

Every day, look at yourself in the mirror - look yourself in the eyes and say, "I love you... really." Utilize this time to reflect on your daily gratitude. It's imperative that you find gratitude for all things, even if you don't feel positive about the situation.

SURROUND YOURSELF WITH POSITIVE PEOPLE

Everything is about relationships. If you truly want change in your life, it's important to be around people with a similar mindset. Don't let other people get you down. When you are feeling down yourself, being around somebody who is laughing and joking will help your mood. Remember that you are worth only the best. Do not stay around "Debbie-Downers."

In chapter 5, I discussed what supportive environments can do for you. Go back and read more about that and make sure you stay around positive people. That can be hard in a workplace, but it is not worth being "polite" and not doing anything about it. Try to interact as little as possible with people who have a negative attitude. If it is your boss who affects you negatively, you have to evaluate the effect this has on you and whether or not you should stay in that workplace. The basic rule is, take responsibility for your situation and for yourself. And again, always strive for win-win relationships, find people who believe in you and inspire you to improve, and surround yourself with people who are supportive of what you are doing.

I previously talked about the importance of who you should associate yourself with. The key to cultivating and maintaining a positive mental attitude is to take control of your thinking and avoid negative minded people.

If you hang around negativity, you will become negative. If you surround yourself with positivity, your life will be positive. Attitudes of others tend to linger within your own self. Negative people remove the enthusiasm we talked about earlier. You need enthusiasm to set that flame within you. Therefore, you want to eliminate all the negative emotions and replace them with positive.

Your job from now on is to be up around people you love. No more complaining.

BE THE POSITIVE ONE

Decide to be the one who is always positive. No more moaning, complaining or grumbling. From now on you are the cheerful, "always up" one, around whom good things revolve and happen. No matter how low, down or fed up you are when asked how you are, you will say "fine, good, marvelous." The interesting thing is that when you answer in a positive way, even if you don't feel it, you will undoubtedly make yourself and everyone around you more upbeat. It really works.

Successful people are invariably cheerful. They think positively, act positively, and project confidence and enthusiasm. Life for all of us can be tough, but someone has to lift the spirits. The beauty is that this will benefit you in so many ways when you do.

I like to go to sleep feeling I've made a difference, been honestly kind and cheerful to people around me, acting out as the positive one, spread a little happiness and had some fun. I work hard to be that person and I can assure you that it "pays off." Play the happy part and you will feel happy. Even though it might feel awkward at first, if you are not used to it, you can do it!

THINK WIN-WIN

The concept of win-win means that agreements are mutually beneficial, mutually satisfying. Win-win is a frame of mind that constantly seeks mutual benefit in all interactions. With a win-win solution, all parties feel good about the decision and feel committed to the action plan.

Win-win is based on the paradigm that there is plenty for everybody. One person's success is not achieved at the expense of the success of others.

POSITIVE HABITS

"Give yourself a powerful positive suggestion every morning. Something that will carry you through the day!"

—Bob Proctor

Do what you need to create positive habits that get you up. It does not need to be habits that are directly related to your Power Goals, but indirectly they will energize you to move you towards your goals. In my life I have a special friend, Jenny. We try to meet and drink coffee every day to support each other in the personal and business matters. Even though we don't meet for very long, we manage to give each other a lot of good inspiration.

Other positive habits I have in my life:

- Going for a long walk every day, to get fresh air and exercise. For me it is like meditation;
- Doing yoga in the morning;
- Having a date with my husband every second week;
- Reading positive material daily, at a specific time;
- Tuesday meeting with my accountability partner, for energy and inspiration;
- Not skipping training;
- Going to the theatre with my girlfriends once a month.

What positive habits do you have?

SELF-CONTROL OVER YOUR EMOTIONS AND REACTIONS

It's a challenging task to develop a calm, focused mind, but well worth the effort.

- **Breath** - When a challenge arises, bring your attention immediately to your breathing, and begin taking long, slow deep breaths in and out through your nose to induce immediate calm and control over your mind and emotional state.

- **Break** - Take a five-minute break and go to a quiet place where you can collect yourself.
- **Smile** – Smiling is a technique. You don't have to feel happy but just by changing your projection and smiling, you can change your mood, energy and feelings, immediately. Practice.
- **Water** - Have a full glass of water when you feel upset, irritated or angry, to shift your energy and balance your system.
- **Affirm** - Mentally repeat the affirmation over and over again: "I am happy…, I am grateful…, I am strong…". Positive affirmations help adjust the hemispheres of the brain by activating different meridian points in the mouth. Repeat this affirmation at least 26 times.
- **Adjust your posture**. Straighten your spine, relax your shoulders, lift your chest, bring your chin in a little and breathe. Straightening your spine will help remove blocked energy in the system as well as allowing the energy to flow naturally, affecting your thoughts, feelings and actions.
- **Take a moment** - to tune into the infinite potential within you. In times of stress, mentally "tune in" to the vibration that you are in. Breathe, tell yourself to relax. Be open to a different perspective. Take the wiser path….consciously.
- **Adjust your self-talk** – say something really nice to yourself!

Positive Actions - Walk The Extra Mile

"An important principle of success in all walks of life and all occupations is a willingness to go the extra mile - which means the rendering of more and better service than that for which one is paid and giving it in a positive mental attitude."

—Napoleon Hill

Over deliver in everything you do. Do the little extra. Give more than you need to. If you look around you will notice that very few walk the extra mile. Like Paula Abdul said: **"There is no traffic beyond the extra mile".** That means, if you put in the extra effort you will be one of the few who stand out.

Sometimes in life we find it difficult to slow down and take the time for someone else. It always seems to be about ourselves; however, if you would take the time for someone who needs it you would see how your own life would change toward the positive. When you give, you get...10x over. It also provides a sense of self-worth when you know that you made a difference in another's life. You can over deliver for a customer, someone in the family or for a charitable organization.

The more you give without expecting anything in return, the more you will get from the most unexpected sources.

Givers Gain is a philosophy based on the law of reciprocity. In the context of networking groups, people who adopt this philosophy dedicate themselves to giving business to their fellow networkers rather than making their foremost concern getting business for themselves.

In doing so, other people naturally become eager to repay their kindness by sending them business in return. Givers Gain is a great way to live life in general and it is a standard which we can all apply to ourselves—key word being "ourselves"; it is not a sword to be pointed at others who may not adopt the philosophy.

Look for opportunities to help someone. It doesn't matter if you know them, but you will soon see that you will win from helping others. Napoleon Hill said that great achievement is usually born of great sacrifice and is never the result of selfishness. It does not matter if you give of your time, your money or your knowledge. What goes around, comes around.

Also, learn to give to yourself. This can sometimes be the hardest giving we need to learn. Filling your own cup up allows you to give to others.

FOCUS ON PLANTING POSITIVE SEEDS IN YOUR LIFE

"I will waste not even a precious second today in anger, or hate, or jealousy or selfishness. I know that the seeds I sow will harvest because every action, good or bad, is always followed by an equal reaction. I will plant only good seeds today."

—Og Mandino

Make up your mind today that if any negative thoughts come to you, you will just reject them. Send them love. I guarantee you will have a good day. And remember, it will make a harvest for a good future.

Don't Let Rejections Get You Down

To be successful you have to be willing to risk rejection. Rejection is a natural part of life. Not everyone can say yes to you, but keep on going and do not let it get you down.

Mark Victor Hansen and Jack Canfield wrote their #1 bestselling *Chicken Soup for the Soul* and their manuscript was rejected 130 times. They did not give up and have now sold 250 million copies.

If the statistics say that only 10% will succeed, that means that 10 out of 100 will say "yes" to your offer. That means every one of the 90 that will say "no" put you closer to the 10 that will say "yes." I was working with a company where we were celebrating every time somebody got a rejection, because that was one step closer to a sale. It was a fun way of keeping the energy up.

Positive Shifters

Have a plan up your sleeve. Make a list of "Shifters" that can change your feelings in a moment. It can be a thought of nature, funny moments, your favorite music, beautiful memories or a person you love; happy thoughts. Something that you know will make you feel good inside and change your mood and energy in a heartbeat.

No matter how hard you have been working, no matter how annoying life has been, no matter how fed up you feel, the gloom will be lifted, and you will be instantly restored, calm and happy.

The things that lift us are generally not the things that cost money. It can be walks on the beach, a favorite book or movie, sitting in the sun, chats with a special friend, your dog, your children, entering into your house or a favorite song that makes you want to dance. Anything that will lift your mood is magical.

What are your positive shifters? Make a list of at least three.

1. _____

2. _____

3. _____

ENTHUSIASM

"Enthusiasm is one of the most powerful engines of success."

— Ralph Waldo Emerson

In the book, *Success through a Positive Mental Attitude* by Napoleon Hill and W. Clement Stone, they say that enthusiasm is absolutely essential for success.

Do you know that most people don't really understand what enthusiasm is? Most people think that enthusiasm is pounding on your chest and yelling and jumping around, but that is not it at all. It is a state of energized calmness. You will find that enthusiastic people don't rush, they don't make a big noise and there is something about them that you are attracted to. Perhaps, it is what is going on inside and it resonates with what goes on inside of you.

Enthusiasm comes from the Greek entheos - in God. That means that intellectually, you are in touch with the essence of who you are, the higher side of your personality.

Be enthusiastic about life and you will express it in your energy. People will pick it up and they will naturally be attracted to you, but most of all you will really like yourself, and that is so important.

Enthusiasm can be developed by doing what you are passionate about. This is worth repeating: Enthusiasm can be developed by doing what you love to do. The most successful people I know are so passionate about what they do, that they would happily do what they do for free. If money was not an issue; what would you do with your life and your time? If you can find this true passion, you will by default be enthusiastic about your life, your goals and your achievements.

When you express enthusiasm to others, you will become a magnet to others, who will be attracted to your high level of energy. Other people will want to work with you, play with you, and support you. As a result you will get more done in less time.

Enthusiasm is such a powerful, powerful word. You can build a business on it, but better than that, you can build a life on it. Ask yourself, "Am I really enthusiastic about my life?"

Be enthusiastic in everything you do and everything you set your mind to.

OPTIMISM

"There are no mistakes, only opportunities to learn from."

— Cleo Robertson

To be an optimistic person is to see every problem as

a great possibility for learning and see possibilities in everything. It is also to find opportunities in every difficulty. I am not saying that it is easy to always think and act in an optimistic way, but it's important.

There are no mistakes – there are only circumstances from which to learn. To be a real winner you have to make many mistakes to learn from. If the Wright brothers had looked at all their crashes as mistakes they would have never succeeded in being the first ones to fly. There is always another way to look at things. To choose one's attitude in any given set of circumstances is to choose one's own way." Your attitude, which includes your thoughts, feelings, and actions, is something you have complete control over today.

Everyone can learn to be an optimist by always seeing the possibilities where everyone else sees the problems. You choose the life you want to live. It does not matter if you are a man or a woman, black or white, thin or heavy, young or old. By focusing on your dreams, Power Goals and staying optimistic, your life will surely change for the better – in all respects. Instead of eliminating worry and anxiety, most of us spend a lot of time doubting things that never even come to pass. To be happier, healthier, and a whole lot wealthier, save worry and anxiety for the major upsets in life. Decide to be optimistic and not let "bumps in the road" get you down.

Always look for the door that is opening, not the one that just closed. As Alexander Graham Bell said, "**When one door closes, another opens, but we so often look so long and regretfully upon the closed door that we do not see the one which opens for us**". An optimistic attitude makes sure that you look for the good that is coming.

Happiness Is A Choice

"Make a conscious effort to see everything in a very positive way and look for the best in every situation."

— Bob Proctor

When I was working as the sales director at the Royal Swedish Theatre, my positivity and optimism were the worst threat to the people around me. It is a lovely 150-year-old building with beautiful architecture. The surroundings are amazing, the product (theatre plays) is great and only the best actors and directors work there. I was excited to work there, but the first thing I came across was how horrible the sales and marketing people perceived their situation. I have never experienced such a negative environment. Instead of focusing on all the good and beauty in their workplace, their choice was to focus on the negative details. In cooperation we made a list of all the problems, all the things that made their situation unbearable. As we started to eliminate the problems on the list, the negative voices around their situation did not become less negative due to the fact that they had chosen to see themselves as victims. No change would make them happier. Again, taking responsibility for a situation is a choice. Just a note, most of them are still working there 20 years later, doing the same job, with the same attitude. Talk about not taking responsibility for your own life.

We can all choose to do certain things every day of

our lives. Some things we do will make us unhappy and some things we choose to do will make us happier. This is the beginning of the rest of your life and only you can choose if you want to be happy or unhappy. Change your mental focus and choose happiness!

IT IS ALL ABOUT ENERGY

Our natural state is to feel good and be happy. It is all about life energy. Energy is the base in everything and the fuel for all living. Positive energy is the key to power within yourself. Use your positive energy to your own development and success, rather than losing power on everything that pulls you down such as jealousy, bitterness, aggression, fear, hatred, revenge, greed, superstition, pigheadedness and other nonsense.

Our life is influenced so much by our energy level. Create a habit to fill up your energy levels since the optimal is to have a stable energy level in the long-term. Create energy for your body and brain by focusing on the four different areas:

- Eat well
- Sleep
- Exercise
- Relax

Focus on the positive since the negative weakens you. We are all about the energy and you get affected by other people's energy. Program your brain with positive images and your subconscious will focus on all the good and nice that is always around you. Stay positive.

- Take responsibility for your own energy and do not let others steal it from you.
- Do not let others rule your life.
- Respect yourself and do what you feel good about.
- Get the power you deserve!
- Always remember that you are as good as anyone you ever meet.
- You are an amazing human being with great potential.

How do you use your energy? When I work with clients who feel that they constantly lose energy at work, I make an easy test. I ask the person to draw one circle and write how their energy is being used "today" and another circle on how "the ideal situation" would be.

The circles can include:
Meetings
Email
Phone calls
Unnecessary discussions
Finding papers
New prospects
Meeting with clients
Stress
Time to reflect
Education
Pure waste of time

FLOW

Happiness at its best is being "in flow." According to Mihaly Csíkszentmihályi, his theory outlines that people are happiest when they are in a state of *flow* — a state of concentration or complete absorption with the activity at hand and the situation. It is a state in which people are so involved in an activity that nothing else seems to matter. The idea of flow is identical to the feeling of being *in the zone* or *in the groove*. The flow state is an optimal state of *intrinsic motivation*, where the person is fully immersed in what they are doing. This is a feeling everyone has at times, characterized by a feeling of great absorption, engagement, fulfillment, and skill.

Flow gives you energized focus and spontaneous joy. Strive for flow and your Power Goals achievement will feel like pure joy!

SUMMARY ON HOW TO STAY POSITIVE

- Stay focused on past successes, instead of letting your inner voice talk about your failures.
- Use your positive energy towards your own development and success, rather than wasting energy on emotions that pull you down.
- Ask yourself what you can do today to really draw the best out of yourself.
- Only use positive words.
- Create a victory log – a written record of your successes.
- Feed your brain with positive messages.
- Socialize only with positive people.
- Find opportunities in every difficulty.
- Believe in yourself, your abilities and what you can do.

- Be open and enthusiastic about the constant changes that occur in life.
- Have a plan up your sleeve.
- Make a list of "Shifters" that can change your feelings in a moment.
- Watch a funny movie.
- Acknowledge your daily successes.
- The more you give the more you get.
- Remember that there are no mistakes.
- Be grateful for all your blessings

You've turned that dream into reality; you've put that plan of action into place; you've acknowledged that there will be turbulence, but you know how to stay positive and energized; Now, it's time to evaluate if you've achieved your Power Goals and … then…CELEBRATE!!!!!!

9
ACHIEVING YOUR GOAL AND CELEBRATION

"Leaders are made, they are not born. They are made by hard effort, which is the price which all of us must pay to achieve any goal that is worthwhile."

— Vince Lombardi

ACHIEVING YOUR GOAL AND CELEBRATION

**"The more you praise and celebrate your life,
the more there is to celebrate in life."**

— Oprah Winfrey

As we come to the final section of Power Goals, I congratulate you for making it all the way to the "end", especially since a majority of books that people start to read are never finished. I thank you for making it to this point.

Now is when we investigate and evaluate how far you have come, comparing to where you were when we started this journey together. And then it's time to celebrate your progress.

To remind you, we have walked through the Power Goal process, including the definition of the starting point (here and now), how to define your Power Goals, creating the picture of what it will be like having achieved your Power Goal, working the limiting beliefs that have been embedded into your subconscious since you were a young child, creating positive support, committing to taking action, addressing internal and external turbulence, and working on a positive attitude to finally achieve and celebrate your Power Goal. We have also talked about responsibility, making choices, visualization, affirmations, self- discipline, persistence, attitude, positive thinking, Masterminding and the ultimate key to unlocking Power goals; gratitude. NOW is the moment to evaluate your Power Goals. We start by doing a self-analysis and then we summarize what has worked and what has not been as successful. By evaluating how well, by percentage, you have achieved your Power Goals, you will get a picture of what more is needed before you have actually achieved what you set out to do.

CELEBRATION

"Celebrate any progress. Don't wait to get perfect."

— Ann McGee Cooper

It is immensely important to celebrate. As we talked about in chapter 3, Creative Imagination, a big cornerstone to achieving your Power Goals is to feel the feeling of the actual celebration as you have achieved your Power Goals. The questions I asked you then were:

1. What emotions will you feel when you have reached your destination, the achievement of the Power Goals?
2. Who will be the first person you tell?
3. What will be the first thing you do when you have achieved your Power Goals?

Like an athlete who is working towards winning at the Olympics and finally wins the gold medal, the celebration part makes all the practice worthwhile and the upcoming four years of practice towards the next Olympics will be both possible and more inspiring.

For most of us the Olympics is not on the horizon, but we have equivalent Power Goals that are life changing and just as important to us as the gold medal is for the athlete. Our goals are no less important to celebrate.

We are mostly pretty bad at acknowledging our

victories. From experience I know how easy it is to just brush it off and move on to the next task, instead of stopping for a moment, looking back on where we started and celebrate how far we have come. How will YOU celebrate achieving your Power Goals? How will YOU celebrate your "Olympic gold medal?" With a true celebration, you will send out a message to the Universe that you are grateful both to yourself and to the people around you who have helped you get to your Power Goal. The feeling of gratitude is what makes the big difference in what your future life will be like.

By celebrating and showing gratitude, we prepare ourselves and the Universe for another round of Power Goals...

ATTITUDE OF GRATITUDE

**"The entire process of mental adjustment
and atonement can be summed up
in one word - gratitude."**

—Napoleon Hill

As we spoke about earlier in the book, gratitude is a powerful source of inspiration and positivity. I am a firm believer that a big key to the achievement of Power Goals is much a result of power gratitude.

In the end, our way of showing gratitude to the power goal process is by celebrating our success. It is actually pretty simple. The more you acknowledge that it is working, the more it will work. It is a most powerful force. Sometimes a simple "thank you" can open doors of opportunity that otherwise would not open. Thanksgiving is ingrained in our nature. We all love to give and receive thanks. So, thank you!

This is a wonderful world and we should get excited about helping other people, and we should be very grateful for the fact that they help us. Think of the people who are responsible for your way of life, because it is other people who give us everything we have. Spend time thinking about the people who you are grateful to, and then thank them: your friends, your clients, your parents, your children. You may send out thank you notes to them all and be sincere and really be grateful for what they are doing for you, helping you get to your Power Goals.

Annual Self-Analysis

Every year companies make a summary of assets and liabilities. I advise you to do the same. Make a self-analysis regarding all areas of your life – work, family, love-relationship, financial situation, housing, recreation, friendships and Power Goals. To once a year give yourself the opportunity to make a summary of what the year has brought to you, works as a valuable tool moving forward.

Answer the following questions and summarize the answers to yourself. Read the questions and state your answers aloud, so you can hear your own voice. If you are not certain about the answers to some of the questions, seek the counsel of those who know you well, especially those who have no motive in flattering you, and see yourself through their eyes.

This self-analysis should give you a moment of self-reflection and it probably gives you an opportunity to clearly see how you operate in life. The experience will be astonishing and will make it feasible for you to change your behavior and habits in the future.

1. Have I been persistent in following my plans through to completion?
2. Have I reached decisions promptly and definitely at a majority of occasions?
3. Have I delivered service of the best possible quality of which I was capable or could I have improved in any way?
4. Have I improved my personality during this year?
5. If yes, in what ways have I improved my personality?
6. Have I been cooperative at all times?
7. Have I operated in a harmonious way, with the people I work with as well as my family?
8. Have I permitted myself to procrastinate?
9. If I have been procrastinating, to what extent?
10. Have I permitted my fears to decrease my efficiency?
11. Do I feel like I take responsibility at all times?
12. Do I stand by the choices I make?
13. Have I created a habit of visualization and affirmations?
14. Do I have self-discipline enough to stay aligned to my daily, weekly and monthly plans?
15. Do I operate with a positive attitude and positive thinking?
16. Do I have a Mastermind group that I can rely on and get energy from?
17. Do I have an accountability partner who helps me to focus on my Power Goals at all times?

18. Do I have a gratitude book to write down all that I have to be grateful for, every day?
19. Have my relationships during the year been pleasant?
20. Has my relationship with any of my associates or family been unpleasant? If so, has the fault been partly, or wholly mine?
21. Have I been open minded and tolerant?
22. Have I increased my ability to help others?
23. Do I make it a habit "to walk the extra mile?"
24. Have I expressed, either openly or secretly, any form of egoism?
25. Have my decisions been respectful towards my associates?
26. Have my decisions been based on accuracy of analysis and thought?
27. Have I made time-plans to fulfill my Power Goals?
28. Have I budgeted my expenses?
29. Have I fulfilled my budget?
30. Have I been unfair to anyone?
31. If so, in what way?
32. Am I in the right profession?
33. Have I changed my habits so that I have become more efficient?
34. How can I improve my habits so that I become even more efficient during the coming year?
35. Am I working to break out of my "box" of limitations so that I explore ideas and options to experience creative breakthroughs?
36. Am I consciously rejecting the limitations of common thinking in order to accomplish uncommon results?

37. Compared to a year ago, how successful do I feel on a scale of 1 to 10?

Ask yourself the following questions regarding last year:

What are the 3 most important things that I have become aware of concerning myself?

1. _____

2. _____

3. _____

What are the 3 most important things that I have achieved last year?

1. _____

2. _____

3. _____

What are the 3 most important areas I need to improve?

1. _____

2. _____

3. _____

Do You Live A Balanced Life?

Investigate how you devote your time to different areas of your life. Find out if you live a balanced life. During a week, how much time out of 112 hours (we assume 8 hours of sleep per night) do you spend on:

1. Your occupation/ work?
2. Your family?
3. Your relationship?
4. Acquiring useful knowledge/ studying?
5. Play and relaxation?
6. Plain waste?

To give you an example of the above, you should devote approximately 35% to work. The remaining 65% should be balanced as equally as possible between the other areas. Except of course plain waste which has no place at all in anybody's life.

To clarify, I have made a distinction between relationship and family since they are both important to nourish. Studying an hour every day is a great key to success, both in your professional life and for your personal development.

And when living a balanced life, it is important to sleep 7-8 hours per night, not forgetting that play and relaxation also should fit into your life.

The 3 things that have surprised me the most are:

1. _____

2. _____

3. _____

If you have answered all of the above questions truthfully, you know more about yourself than the majority of people in the world. Most likely you have learned major things about yourself, you know what you have achieved and you know what you need to focus on during the coming year.

EVALUATE YOUR POWER GOAL ACHIEVEMENT

This is the moment to evaluate your Power Goals. In the beginning of the book I explained to you about the 9 steps that we were going to take. To remind you, these are the steps:

You have already made a self-analysis and then you have summarized what has worked and what has not been so successful.

How well have you achieved your Power Goals?

The aim is to have achieved a 100% success with what you set out to do when you started this process.

Has it been totally fulfilled or do you have a gap to fill? If so, how will you be able to fill that gap? Can you do it by yourself or do you need the help from somebody else? A close friend, a colleague at work, a professional coach or somebody else?

Ask yourself, have I attained my Power Goals which I established as my objective for this year?

My goal fulfillment for Power goal #1:

_____% (out of 100%)

My goal fulfillment for Power goal #2:

_____% (out of 100%)

My goal fulfillment for Power goal #3:

_____% (out of 100%)

IF NOT 100% GOAL ACHIEVEMENT

"Go from good to great. Greatness is not primarily a function of circumstance, but largely a matter of conscious choice, and discipline."

—Jim Collins

If you did not get to a 100% achievement of your Power Goals, you should still celebrate that you got as far as you did and that counts for a lot. Do not be too hard on yourself. Instead, celebrate that you did get much further than you were last year and that you have been persistent in your activities. Celebrate the focus even more on your Power Goals. Celebrate that you have been open minded, operated out of your comfort zone, challenged yourself, learned and anything else that counts towards your progress.

Realize that some Power Goals can be hard to achieve in only one year. Celebrate that you got as far as you did. If one of your Power Goals is to find a new love relationship and during the time you set up for yourself you have still not found the right person, but you have opened up for a new relationship and you have been on several dates, it also counts.

Celebrate all your successes!

In case you have NOT reached 100% fulfillment of your Power Goals, what in particular do you need to do or what support do you need in order to reach 100%?

Power goal #1: _____

Power goal #2: _____

Power goal #3: _____

You can see this as the equivalent to ending up as number four in the Olympics. Do you think that athlete would give up and not try to win again?

EXCUSES FOR NOT ACHIEVING YOUR POWER GOALS

"It has always been a mystery to me why people spend so much time deliberately fooling themselves by creating alibis to cover their weaknesses."

— Elbert Hubbard

Unfortunately, some of you have not been able to achieve your Power Goals due to lack of persistence or lack of focus. Statistics say that only a small percentage achieve what they set out to achieve. If you did not achieve your Power Goal fully, did you have an excuse for not doing so?

So many people allow themselves to have excuses and here are some of them. Examine yourself carefully if you hide behind any of these alibis.

- If I only had money...

- If I had a good education...
- If I could only get a job...
- If I only had more time...
- If only the economy was different...
- If I had been given a chance...
- If I were only younger...
- If I had been born rich...
- If I could only meet the "the right people"...
- If times were better...
- If I had good health...
- If my boss appreciated me...
- If I lived in a big city...
- If I could just get started...
- If I were not so overweight...
- If I hadn't lost all of my money...
- If luck were not against me...
- If other people would only listen to me...
- If I were sure of myself...
- If I did not have a wife and kids to support...
- If I could only get out of debt...
- If I did not have to work so hard...
- If I had the talent that some people have...
- If I only had somebody to help me...
- If I only did not have writer's block...
- If I...

If you hide behind any one of these excuses you position yourself as a victim. As we talked about in chapter 7 (Expect Turbulence) you will never achieve your goals if you allow yourself to be a victim and feel sorry for yourself. Once again, it is crucial to take full responsibility for your own life.

Alibis with which to explain away failure is fatal to success. Building alibis is a deeply rooted habit and as we've talked about, habits are difficult to break especially when they prove justification for something we do.

If you have the courage to see yourself as you really are and the alibis you provide for yourself, you have the possibility to correct what is wrong and learn from the experience. Now is the time to look over your Power Goals one more time and ask yourself if you are really willing to work hard to achieve them.

CELEBRATE YOURSELF

"Our deepest fear is not that we are inadequate. Our deepest fear is that we are powerful beyond measure. We ask ourselves: Who am I to be brilliant, gorgeous, talented, fabulous? Actually, who are you not to be?"

— Marianne Williamson

Celebrate what you want to see more of. Celebrate your success. Congratulate yourself. Celebrate that you got as far as you did. Receive compliments well. Allow yourself to shine. Allow yourself to be brilliant. Allow yourself to continue to challenge yourself by setting new and wonderful Power Goals. And continue to celebrate all your successes.

Enhance the pleasure of success and give yourself the pleasure to acknowledge what you have been able to achieve and praise it.

What do you like about yourself? What is really good about you? What do you do really well? What can you recognize? I am not talking about going on an ego trip. I am talking about the healthy conscious appreciation for who you are. Focusing on what you do well is what will inspire you to do whatever you are doing even better.

We all do some great things and other people will be able to tell you what you do great. Get to the point where you can identify the things that YOU know you do well. Ask yourself; "What are the things that I do well?" Then, to get the question answered from a different perspective, ask other people, "What is it that I do well?" It is a great exercise that I encourage you all to do. Most often than not, we do some great things but as most people do not like to "blow their own trumpet", they never actually give themselves credit for the things that they do really well and this keeps them "thinking small" and usually underachieving. You may be a great connector, great with money, a great student, an excellent motivator, an inspiring communicator or an amazing mom. Take time out to think and consider and review what you do well. It is not being conceited or egotistical, it is identifying what you do well so you can convert what you do "well" into what you do "great."

EXCUSES FOR NOT CELEBRATING

"As a songwriter, there is nothing better than winning 'song of the year'. But I couldn't really celebrate, because it wasn't right. Luther wasn't standing next to me, to receive the award."

— Richard Marx

Why do many of us find it so hard to celebrate? Even little things are worth celebrating, but so many times we just "brush it off" and pretend it was no big effort, even though it was. Instead we just get on with the next task, practically without even breathing in between.

Do you allow yourself to celebrate? People around us are in general not as giving when it comes to personal celebration. As we talked about in the chapter on "external turbulence" close relatives and friends can at times be more jealous than happy for you. This is a general trend in society, except in sports.

The same achievement, but in different settings, is not necessarily celebrated the same way. What do I mean by that? Well, if you run the New York marathon and everybody is cheering when you reach the finish line, it is probably easier for you to celebrate than it would be if you ran the same distance, by yourself, in the woods and nobody was there to cheer when you made that huge accomplishment. It is easier to celebrate when you are with other people, when you have an accountability partner or when you have actually told people about your Power Goals.

CELEBRATE PEOPLE WHO HELPED YOU

"We are powerful creative beings who determine our future with every thought we think and every word we speak."

—Louise Hay

Make people stars and show your appreciation in public. It's motivating for anyone to be recognized for work done well. Praise the people who helped you on your way. Praise them at any time, especially in front of others by making them into a star through applause and a standing ovation.

When someone on your team has a big success, celebrate it and tell others. As Richard Branson says: "Success breeds success."

QUANTUM LEAP

Definition of Quantum Leap

"Making an explosive jump by taking a risk and going off into an unchartered territory with no guide to follow."

— Fred Alan Wolf

By setting and achieving your Power Goals, you can make a quantum leap by doubling or tripling your level of success. If you have achieved your Power Goals by 100%, you have most probably reached a quantum leap. Maybe you did not even know about quantum leaps before you started reading this book and now you've done it!

As Price Prichett explains in his book, you2, most of us think that we must move systematically from our present level of achievement to the next in a gradual process. This is an unfortunate misconception. You can make an "explosive jump" in your personal performance that puts you far beyond the next logical step.

By setting a Power Goal and following the steps in this book, you go for a breakthrough. It is the high-velocity moves that carry you to dramatically higher performance without a time consuming struggle. A quantum leap produces a dramatic and multiple gain, an incremental increase.

You can transform your life into anything that you choose as long as you are really clear on what you want. You do not need to know HOW you're going to get there, but you need to know WHERE you want to go. It is crucial to have a crystal clear picture of what you want to accomplish. And you did have a clear picture when you set your Power Goals. And you did have a clear picture of what you wanted to accomplish. And you did **reach your** quantum leap. All I want to do is congratulate you for making it all this way.

"You've gotta dance like there's nobody watching, Love like you'll never be hurt, Sing like there's nobody listening, And live like it's heaven on earth."

—William W. Purkey

The one asset we all have in common is TIME. It all depends on how we use that time. Don't waste your own precious years. You cannot afford to let another day slip into eternity, without planning your Power Goals and how to achieve them. Life is beautiful and you should always make the most of it. Go out there and excel! Since you have made it this far I know that you can become more successful than you ever dreamed of.

It is with Power Goals as with everything else. The more you practice, the easier it will get. Generally it will become easier to define and achieve your Power Goals from now and onwards. I want to encourage you to set new Power Goals in the future because you can recall the wonderful feeling of achievement. It is about enhancing the pleasure of success.

Thank you for reading my book. I hope it has helped you on this journey we call life. My hope for you is a life of setting and achieving powerful, inspiring goals.

— Prepare to be successful and live life fully!

With love and gratitude,

Christina Sleyth

EXTRA BONUSES

As an EXTRA BONUS, get the Webinar *"Two goal achieving experts discuss - Goal Achieving MAX"* The New York Times Best Selling Author Peggy McColl and Christina discuss what is the most effective, fastest way to achieve any powerful goal. **powergoalsacademy.com/inside-the-book-bonus**

Sign up for FREE WEEKLY INSPIRATION from Christina at **www.oneminuteinspiration.com**

If Power Goals makes a difference to you, I would love to hear from you. I'm always interested in hearing about your Power Goals, so please share on my Facebook page at **www. facebook.com/powergoalsacademy**

You can also read my blog on **www.powergoalsacademy.com**

Acknowledgements

This book is a significant landmark in my life. My heart is overflowing with appreciation and gratitude for every person who has come into my life and inspired and touched me through their presence.

I would like to start by appreciating my family who have been so supportive and understanding during this challenging period of creating this book. To my loving husband Niclas – thank you for coming into my life. My beautiful spiritual children Alexandra and Emma are such precious jewels and illuminate every breath I take through their mere existence. To my special "bonus-children" Beatrice and Rickard, who I am so grateful to have in my life. Thank you to my extraordinary parents Birgit and Torsten who taught me so much and are now in another dimension. I would also like to express my gratitude to my very special parents in-law Inger and Ingemar, who have always treated me as their own daughter.

My gratitude also includes my "American family," the Whites. Bill and Karen allowed me into their family as an exchange student in 1981-1982. This not only gave me three "sisters" – Kristin, Andrea and Susan, but also a new perspective on life, psychology and growth. I would especially like to thank Kristin for all the valuable help in proofreading my book.

Since I have been greatly inspired by my wonderful like-minded friends and teachers in this field, I would like to take the opportunity to acknowledge them.

I am forever grateful to Gil Thompson who got me started on "this road" in 1995 by asking me crucial questions and gifting me with books like James Allen: As a Man Thinketh, Florence Scovel Shinn; "How to Play the Game of Life" and Stephen R. Covey: "7 Habits of Highly Effective People."

I would like to thank Carrie Greschner, my dear friend and inspiration in Canada. Our trips to Sanoviv have been amazing, healing and fun. I would never have experienced so much about myself had you not been there. Thank you for staying in my life!

I am exceptionally grateful to Jill Hutchinson, my Australian – South African accountability partner who inspires me every day and always asks the "right" questions. It feels like we are so close in both mind and location, even though we are so far away in distance. Jill, thank you for being my soul sister.

A huge thanks to Peggy Caruso who is on a special journey together with me. We have supported each other through trainings in Toronto, Arizona and New York. She is an amazing writer, with two books written already and the third on its way. Peggy's help in writing *Power Goals* has been invaluable.

I am grateful to the talented psychologist Villemo Rantzén who "carried" me through the tough years. I am also grateful to Liliana Semjonow who was my mentor for over 15 years. Thank you for all of your wonderful knowledge and insights that you have generously shared.

My story of becoming an expert was started by learning from incredible teachers like Wayne Dyer, Shakti Gawain, Louise Hay, Leo Buscaglia, Bob Proctor, John Gray, Deepak Chopra, Jack Canfield, Paolo Coelho, Mary Morrissey, Christiane Northrup, Sanna Ehdin, Caroline Myss, Rhonda Byrne, Bill Harris, Brian Tracy, and Brendon Burchard. I am forever grateful for your guidance and I am honored to count some of you as friends. Your voice and wisdom have inspired me and sowed the seed for this book.

I am exceptionally grateful to my mentor Bob Proctor, leading man in "The Secret" the #1 International Bestselling author; "You Were Born Rich". Before anyone ever called personal development an industry, Bob was leading the way. Bob is an extraordinarily inspiring man and has personally transformed my life through his teachings, especially during several Matrixx in Toronto. Thank you for the beautiful, kind words in the foreword to this book. I am forever grateful to you.

A special thanks to Jack Canfield, 40 times a New York Times Bestselling Author, among the titles, "The Success Principles" and "Chicken Soup for the Soul." Thank you Jack for your generosity in sharing your personal experiences. Your inspirational speaking and *Breakthrough to Success* training has been crucial for me in writing this book.

I would like to thank my Mastermind Group, "The International Brain Trust," consisting of Mike Mack, Edmonton, Canada; Sawan Kapoor, New Delhi, India;

Nilesh Rathi, Pune, India; Bob Urichuck, Ottawa, Canada and Peggy Caruso, PA, USA. We create miracles together. I am convinced that every meeting is meant to be, for different reasons and learning. The friends I have are definitely in my life for a reason. In no order of preference I would like to particularly mention a few especially important friends that have contributed to my book; Jenny Eriksson, because of our amazing conversations, our great coffee breaks and being there when it is most needed. Cecilia Ålander, for being a true friend to me in everything I go through. Stina Byström who is like a sister and our time together continues to be filled with so much care and trust. Maria Unghanse, who is such a generous person, has given me a great deal of support in encouraging me to keep on writing. And thanks to all of the rest of my fantastic friends; you know who you are!

ABOUT THE AUTHOR

Christina Skytt is the founder of Power Goals Academy, top executive coach and inspirational speaker. Christina has earned a MBA of International Business from the Stockholm School of Economics.

After a long career in the corporate world as a senior executive, Christina became a serial entrepreneur in 2002. She is devoted to the development of organizations by empowering people through the life-changing process of setting and achieving Power Goals. Her clients have included hundreds of executives and entrepreneurs around the globe, among them Apple, Carlsberg, East Capital, Electrolux, Ericsson, Oriflame, Pfizer, Vattenfall and Wyeth.

Christina lives with her husband and their four children in Stockholm, Sweden.